Afro-Americans in California

AFRO-AMERICANS IN CALIFORNIA

Rudolph Lapp
College of San Mateo

series editors:
Norris Hundley, jr.
John A. Schutz

Boyd & Fraser Publishing Company
San Francisco

AFRO-AMERICANS IN CALIFORNIA

Rudolph M. Lapp

© copyright 1979 by Rudolph M. Lapp, c/o Boyd & Fraser Publishing Company, 3627 Sacramento Street, San Francisco, CA 94118. All rights reserved.

Manufactured in the United States of America.

Library of Congress Cataloging in Publication Data:

Lapp, Rudolph M
  Afro-Americans in California.

  Includes bibliographical references.
    1. Afro-Americans—California—History. 2. California—Race relations.
I. Title.
E185.93.C2L35   979.4'004'96073   79-17918
ISBN 0-87835-094-2

1 2 3 4 5 · 3 2 1 0 9

EDITORS' INTRODUCTION

MENTION THE NAME CALIFORNIA and the popular mind conjures up the same images of romance and adventure that prompted the Spaniards in the 1540s to name the locale after a legendary Amazon queen. State of mind no less than geographic entity, California has become a popular image of a wonderful land of easy wealth, better health, pleasant living, and unlimited opportunities. While this has been true for some, for others it has been a land of disillusionment, and for too many it has become a place of crowded cities, congested roadways, smog, noise, racial unrest, and other problems. Still, the romantic image has persisted to make California the most populated state in the Union and the home of more newcomers each day than came during the first three hundred years following discovery by Europeans.

For most of its history California has been shrouded in mystery, better known for its terrain than for its settlers—first the Indians who arrived at least 11,000 years ago and then the Spaniards who followed in 1769. Spaniards, Mexicans, and blacks added only slightly to the non-Indian population until the American conquest of 1846 ushered in an era of unparalleled growth. With the discovery of gold, the building of the transcontinental railroad, and the development of crops and cities, people in massive numbers from all parts of the world began to inhabit the region. Thus California became a land of newcomers where a rich mixture of cultures pervades.

Fact and fiction are intertwined so well into the state's traditions and folklore that they are sometimes difficult to separate. But close scrutiny reveals that the people of California have made many solid contributions in land and water use, conservation of resources, politics, education, transportation, labor organization, literature, architectural styles, and learning to live with people of different cultural and ethnic heritages. These contributions, as well as those instances when Californians performed less admirably, are woven into the design of the Golden

State Series. The volumes in the Series are meant to be suggestive rather than exhaustive, interpretive rather than definitive. They invite the general public, the student, the scholar, and the teacher to read them not only for digested materials from a wide range of recent scholarship, but also for some new insights and ways of perceiving old problems. The Series, we trust, will be only the beginning of each reader's inquiry into the past of a state rich in historical excitement and significant in its impact on the nation.

Norris Hundley, jr.
John A. Schutz

CONTENTS

CHAPTER ONE

Conquest and Gold

EVEN BEFORE CALIFORNIA became part of the United States, blacks had been active in its history. At the outset their experience can be described as the impact of the West on blacks, for blacks were part of the vast movement toward the Pacific Coast in which the determining factors were larger than themselves. Racism, of course, was ever present in American history, even where blacks were few in number. With the great demographic changes precipitated by World War II one can turn the phrase around and speak of the impact of blacks on western history. This essay describes both periods.

Spanish colonial expansion forcibly brought Africans into the New World and started them on their first steps toward California and their new status as Afro-Americans. The sixteenth-century exploratory voyages of the Spanish took innumerable blacks to the New World as members of the crews. Estevanico, or Black Stephen, is the best known of these newcomers. His wanderings with Cabeza de Vaca in the Mississippi Valley and the Southwest are part of that region's history. Less glamorous, but of greater importance in this early period, was the arrival of increasing numbers of slaves to Mexico, then called New Spain. They became an important ingredient in the Spanish founding of Baja California in the seventeenth century, and in the eighteenth century they were among the founders of the pueblo of Los Angeles in 1781. Following the pattern of their Mexican experience, they lost their identity as Afro-Americans in Spanish California through the process of intermarriage with Indian and Spanish peoples. By the nineteenth century Afro-Americans in California were identifying themselves as Mexicans, but such prominent families as Tapia and Pico were known for their African ancestry.[1]

During California's Mexican period, roughly the twenty-five years after 1820, the first known Afro-Americans arrived from the United States. They were often men of the sea who sailed into the Pacific area as crew members on commercial vessels, mostly whalers from New England. They were a handful in number, and like their white counterparts, most were probably deserters who jumped ship to pursue what appeared to be an agreeable life in slow-moving, Mexican California where racism was minimal. What could not have been more than several dozen black men were scattered throughout California and did not constitute a black community. The best known was Allen B. Light, a former seaman who, after he integrated into California society by becoming a Catholic (an absolute requirement for black or white), became an official responsible for suppressing the illegal otter hunting along the Santa Barbara Coast.[2]

Another prominent Afro-American immigrant of this period was Alexander Leidesdorff, whose African ancestry was unknown until after his death in 1848. This maritime merchant of Danish and West Indian black ancestry first went into business as a white man in New Orleans and then in 1841 came to San Francisco where he resumed his career as an export-import merchant. He also took a leading role in San Francisco's community life and was a central force in starting schools for children.[3] Further evidence that he was not known as an Afro-American was his appointment as a vice-consul for the United States by the Democratic President James K. Polk just prior to the American occupation of California in 1846. Jacob W. Harlan, an Indianan who migrated to California before the gold rush, became well acquainted with Leidesdorff. Many years later, when he and others learned of Leidesdorff's black ancestry, Harlan wrote, "Instead of having his name given to the little street which bears it, he deserved to have one of the chief streets named for him."

American occupation brought many newcomers to California and with them additional blacks. Military officers of southern origin took along their servants, who may have been slaves as well. Government officials did likewise and, when the wives of these military and government personnel arrived, they frequently had black servants of both sexes. One available statistic tells us that by 1847 there were ten blacks in San Francisco and fewer than ten in Monterey, which was still the center of northern California's social and political life.[4] Arriving monthly were also black servants of both sexes who came with the business and professional men who were anticipating commercial opportunities in the West and needed help in setting up their enterprises.

In black history east of the Mississippi River there were periods of free black migration to the various western frontiers during the pre–gold rush years, but these migrations did not signify large movements of people. Legislation in the free states at that time discouraged the migration of blacks to the West. For free blacks to migrate to western slave states would indicate they were incredibly uninformed. There is little record that this ever happened. Abolitionist and Afro-American newspapers in the East kept blacks fully informed about racial prejudice in western free states. When California became part of the United States, these journals indicated that this new territory would be equally uninviting for people of color. Some editors even predicted that the new territory would join the slave states, a position they steadily held until 1848.

In January of that year gold was discovered on the American River. For the first weeks men tried to keep the secret, but within a few months northern California was ablaze with excitement. For a brief period San Francisco and Monterey became ghost towns. Since both ports were now part of the United States, many commercial fleets flying the stars and stripes stopped at those towns. As their crews heard stories of gold, vessels rapidly became ghost ships. There were scores or perhaps even hundreds of blacks among these crews, especially aboard the New England whalers. Most headed quickly for the Mother Lode country along with their white compatriots. There were a few blacks associated with military and naval contingents who preceded the eastern black seamen into the gold fields, but the latter constituted the largest group of black gold miners.

By the end of 1848 word of this dramatic discovery had

reached the eastern states and preparations for the historic 1849
gold rush were well under way. Blacks were part of that remarkable migration. Coastal city free blacks, many from Massachusetts as well as New York, Pennsylvania and Maryland, came
largely by the Panama route and some around the Horn. From
the upper Mississippi valley states many earned their way as employees of the overland companies. From the slave states hundreds of blacks came with their gold-hunting masters, some
with the promise of freedom in California if the rewards of mining were great enough. By 1850 there were 962 Afro-Americans
in California, mostly in the Mother Lode counties, probably
about half of them slaves.[5]

During these early years of the gold rush blacks remained
scattered and enjoyed very little community life. Still, there
were those blacks of the free Negro communities of the northern states who regarded California more as an opportunity for
profitable business and employment opportunities than as a
place for successful gold mining. Mifflin Wistar Gibbs, the Philadelphia black abolitionist, is an example. Not long after his
arrival in San Francisco, he formed a partnership with a fellow
black Philadelphian in a boot and shoe business that prospered.

As early as 1849 it was apparent that California would not
become a slave state, and while that area's laws reflected racist
attitudes, there was a widespread belief that California's economic possibilities were limitless and available to anyone. Even
the black and abolitionist press reported blacks doing well in the
West. For instance, the Philadelphia black community read in
their local antislavery paper that two blacks had returned home
in 1851 with $30,000 after only four months in the diggings. As
a result, free blacks in greater numbers were attracted to California, and by 1852 more than two thousand Afro-Americans
were living in the state. Most of these people were engaged or
employed in business and congregated in San Francisco, Sacramento, Marysville, and Stockton, in that order. In time, they
were among the leaders of their communities.

Southern California during the gold rush decade grew much
more slowly than northern California, but it held its population
in spite of attractions elsewhere. A handful of blacks could be
found scattered throughout this southern region with a half

"Andy at the Sluice." A photo taken at the Auburn ravine in 1852. (*Reprinted by permission of the Bancroft Library, University of California, Berkeley.*)

dozen of them in <u>Los Angeles</u>. They were engaged in various menial and farming occupations. Illustrative of the Afro-Americans who would eventually achieve standing in Los Angeles were Peter Biggs, who had a booming business as a barber; Biddy Mason, who won her freedom in a celebrated court case; and Robert Owens, whose subsequent material success in real estate gave the name "Owens Block" to property at Broadway near Third Street. However, black institutions would not become clearly visible until the end of the century.

Churches were the first black organizations to develop. By 1852, San Francisco had both a black Methodist and Baptist church. While some blacks attended the major white churches, the deep urge for independence in religious matters brought the overwhelming majority of Afro-Americans into their own churches. Before the decade was over, there were black churches in Sacramento, Marysville, and Stockton. In Grass Valley a small but sturdy church was flourishing, with members who were largely ex-slaves.

During the decade before the Civil War, the black population
in California was overwhelmingly male. But family life gradually
developed and young children reached school age. In 1854
schools were opened for black children in San Francisco and
Sacramento. In San Francisco, the African Methodist Episcopal
church founded its own school and in Sacramento some black
families pooled their resources to set up a private school. California at this time did little for school children and nothing for
black school children. Then, toward the end of the decade, the
state legislature allowed counties and cities to provide funds for
segregated schools and black families began to see some return
of their tax money. By that time church basement schools could
be found in Marysville and Stockton as well. The teachers in the
early years were usually A.M.E. and black Baptist clergymen.
Among them were accomplished men like the New Bedford–
born Jeremiah B. Sanderson, who had struggled successfully for
integrated education in his native Massachusetts. The struggle
for adequate and integrated schools was not energetically and
successfully mounted until after the Civil War, after much racist
treatment by the authorities and in much of the press.[6]

While many blacks, like many whites, remained gold miners
until the end of the 1850s, the center of economic and social life
soon became the four major cities of northern California. It was
here that employment and material accumulation were possible
in a significant way. By the middle of this decade there were
scores of blacks in successful businesses and trades. A great
number worked as seamen, cooks, stewards and in other occupations related to food and service employment. The ever-
increasing San Francisco Bay shipping and passenger traffic was
a source of much black income. Many also found work in a great
variety of menial occupations. It was soon clear that Afro-
Americans in California were matching, if not exceeding, the
wealth of their counterparts in the eastern states and at a faster
rate. As propertied persons they became increasingly concerned
that the law protect their property as well as their persons. But
California's laws fell short of their needs.

Like most other northern free states, California's 1849 constitution did not provide blacks with either the vote or the right
to give testimony in court. This latter discrimination was most

threatening to black property rights as well as to their personal safety. If blacks were robbed, and if there were only black witnesses, no matter how many, and no willing white witnesses, the injured blacks had no recourse to the law. The aforementioned Mifflin Wistar Gibbs was among those victimized by this racist feature of the law. He and his partner were robbed of a pair of expensive boots in broad daylight in their shop by two whites who walked off laughing. This unjust law was the spur to the biggest black civil rights struggle of the 1850s. It produced the California Colored Convention movement and three petition campaigns to amend the state's testimony law.[7]

Experienced black leadership in the struggle for equal testimony rights was readily available. Many of the transplanted black easterners, while all quite young, had been leaders in the abolitionist movement, in the state colored convention movements, and in their churches. The roster included men like William H. Hall, William H. Yates, Peter Anderson, J. H. Townsend, Henry Collins, Mifflin W. Gibbs, and the Reverends T. M. D. Ward, J. J. Moore, and J. B. Sanderson. Gibbs later held responsible public office under post–Civil War Republican administrations. Younger men, such as Edward Duplex from New Haven, Connecticut, rose rapidly into the California black leadership class. Many of these men had been associated with Frederick Douglass and William Lloyd Garrison in eastern struggles. They were articulate and educated. A few had studied at Oberlin College in Ohio. Their presence in California testified to their energy and initiative.

In 1852, some of the earlier black settlers from San Francisco organized a Franchise League, the initial force in the struggle for equal rights in offering court testimony. They and blacks from Sacramento conducted a petition campaign that was ignored by the Democrats who controlled the state legislature. Between 1852 and 1855 the black community continued to grow by immigration, and the number of leaders increased as well. The year 1855 witnessed another effort to revise the testimony laws. That year the American (Know Nothing) party won the state elections and the governorship as well. Among the party's leaders were individuals, including some newspaper owners, whom blacks considered friends of their cause. The increasing black interest in politics led in 1855 to the First California Colored Convention. The statewide gathering took place in Sacramento in November.

This three-day convention agreed on an energetic petition campaign that would concentrate on white supporters and appeal for justice for the highly literate black minority. Other subjects reached the convention floor, but the delegates felt that the right to offer testimony was more important in their present plans than suffrage or education. Discussion about a black weekly newspaper also arose, but action was postponed. The debate did result in the founding during the next year of the *Mirror of the Times*. The petition committees gathered thousands of signatures, but they were rejected by a disdainful legislature. Despite this disappointment, the convention executive committee agreed to try again through a second convention.[8]

In December 1856 the Second Colored Convention met, and again in Sacramento. It had been heralded in September of that year by the appearance of California's first black weekly newspaper, the *Mirror of the Times*. As the official organ of the convention movement, the weekly was edited by William H. Newby and Jonas Townsend. (About fifty or sixty issues were published before the newspaper expired in January 1858. Only three numbers are known to exist today.) Financial support of the *Mirror* was an important topic of the second convention proceedings but the convention's main concern continued to be the fight for equal testimony rights. A second petition campaign was mounted but it too was rejected by the state legislature, although a bit more politely. This campaign was marked by an awkward problem that faced the black petitioners. The California constitution denied equal testimony rights to Chinese and Indians as well as blacks. While missionaries decried the injustice to the Chinese, blacks knew that many of their white supporters would not push for testimony rights for Chinese and Indians, so they confined their work to their own group. The expression "third world solidarity" would not be heard until over a hundred years later.

The events of 1857 did not heighten the spirits of the California black community as far as their fight for civil rights was concerned. Nationally the Dred Scott decision had been handed down by the Supreme Court; in California their petition cam-

paign suffered rejection a second time; and soon a number of
their friends in state politics, including Governor J. Neely Johnson, would be defeated at the polls. In spite of these setbacks,
the call went out for a third convention to assemble in San Francisco early in October 1857.

Delegates discovered quickly that the major issues of the convention were the petition campaign to democratize the testimony laws, the need for support for the *Mirror of the Times,* and
the lack of educational opportunities for black children. These
issues and others, all reflecting the continued growth of the
black community, were to receive major attention in 1858, but
other concerns now pressed on them. A rabidly anti-black state
legislature unexpectedly introduced an anti-black immigration
bill with vicious and humiliating features in it which reflected
the emotion generated from California's most famous fugitive
slave case.

The Archy Lee trial in 1858 stands apart from other fugitive
slave cases in California. Before the voters in California had out-
lawed slavery in the constitution of 1849, hundreds of black
men had been brought by their masters to the state in order to
mine gold. As this provision of the constitution became known,
some masters returned to the slave states with their slaves. But
many continued to come, feeling certain that nothing would
happen to their "property." Still others came with their slaves
to whom they promised freedom after a certain amount of gold
had been dug, usually $2,000 worth. It was not long before
some blacks began to take matters into their own hands and flee
to freedom within the boundaries of this free state. Upon recap-
ture, the courts came into the picture. Some judges freed blacks,
stating that the national Fugitive Slave Law of 1850 did not
apply to those who fled slavery within California's boundaries.
This prompted the state legislature, which was largely friendly
to slave owners, to pass a temporary fugitive slave law to ensure
possession for slave owners planning to return to the slave states
with their slaves. The new law was passed in 1852 and was annu-
ally renewed until 1856 when it was allowed to expire. In January 1858, a young Mississippian named Stovall brought his family slave, Archy Lee, to Sacramento. Eighteen-year-old Lee,
influenced by activist free blacks in the town, struck for free-

"ARCHY."

TO THE FRIENDS

......OF THE......

CONSTITUTION AND LAWS.

THE COMMITTEE APPOINTED BY THE
Colored People having expended a large amount, and in-
curred heavy obligations in prosecuting and defending the case
in the Courts of Sacramento, Stockton and San Francisco, and
believing the principles to be vindicated are those which should
interest all lovers of right and justice, independent of com-
plexion, respectfully solicit contributions for this object, which
will be faithfully appropriated, if left with
    m20-3t   E. J. JOHNSON, 184 Clay street.

"Archy." An advertisement in the *California Chronicle,* San Francisco, 1858.

dom. He was shortly apprehended, and for four months, from
January to April 1858, the state was aroused by the struggle
conducted by the black community and its white allies to free
Archy Lee. What made the case untypical was the state Supreme
Court's decision, in spite of the law, to hand Lee back to slavery
because his owner was "young and inexperienced"! From coast
to coast the press ridiculed California's Supreme Court. The ad-
verse publicity may have affected the outcome of the case, but
one more scene remained to be played out.

The final phase of the case took place before the United States
Commissioner. This southern-born federal appointee, William
Penn Johnston, received the case (though reluctantly) because
Stovall's desperate lawyers had been defeated in the San Francisco courts. Their last hope was that this southerner would in-
terpret the federal Fugitive Slave Law of 1850 as legal justifica-
tion for returning Archy Lee to slavery. Johnston certainly knew

in advance that the case did not come under his jurisdiction, but, undoubtedly for political reasons, he agreed to hear it. After weeks of courtroom drama, the commissioner declared that the Fugitive Slave Law did not apply to Archy Lee because he had not crossed state lines in his flight from slavery. Archy Lee went free.

The Archy Lee case contributed to the state legislative fever when a bill to ban black immigration almost became law in 1858. The case also deflected to some extent the work of the Third Colored Convention. Black energies became so involved in the details and excitement of the Archy Lee case that the petition campaign for equal testimony rights suffered. Yet many names were collected and presented to the state legislature, which rejected them for a third time.

The political situation in California discouraged plans for a fourth colored convention. The Republican party, which nationally contained the only friends of the blacks and which had grown rapidly in the East and North, was still very small in the West. The few covert friends whom blacks had in the Democratic party were deeply embroiled in inner party rivalries. The Archy Lee victory was the only bright spot for blacks in 1858 in California.

By spring of 1858 hundreds of California Afro-Americans were on their way to Victoria, British Columbia, and the Fraser River gold rush of that year. The business and job opportunities in British Columbia, plus the promise of dignity and respect in the Queen's colony, provided an escape from the personal frustrations of California life. Among those who left were many who were economically well off but anxious for a less racist atmosphere. The records suggest that most of these migrants to California did well in their new status, and some of them, like Mifflin Wistar Gibbs, eventually became elected officials in Victoria. When the Civil War began in 1861, many returned to California and even to the eastern states.

The departure of the migrants to Canada did not make a very serious dent in the black population of California. By 1860, there were still nearly five thousand Afro-Americans, some of them West Indians, scattered throughout the state and in the four major cities of northern California. In 1859, the silver discoveries in Nevada attracted some blacks to that area, but the numbers were not significant. While more went to the Comstock silver regions in the next decade and a trickle of black migration to California resumed in this same period, the black population in the 1860s remained short of five thousand.

During the Civil War western blacks participated as an integral part in the economic life of the region. As members of a minority group, they still suffered from civil rights discrimination and racist cultural oppression, but economically they were comfortable. Much of the racism of California at this time concentrated against the Indians and the Chinese, by far the larger minority groups. Blacks were still but one percent of the state's population.

When actual fighting between the North and the South began in April 1861, there was a surge of hope among blacks in the North that slavery was doomed and that their position in American life would improve. But Abraham Lincoln's emphasis upon union instead of abolition in the early phase of the war was disappointing. He assured the South that he had no intention of impairing slavery where it already existed, and the United States Army rejected free blacks who wished to enlist in the war against the South. These positions dashed the hopes of northern blacks and, during the latter part of 1861 and the first half of 1862, their mood was largely pessimistic. Black public opinion in California does not become clear until the founding of the *Appeal,* the successor to the *Mirror of the Times.* The birth of the *Appeal* in 1862 was primarily due to the presence of Phillip A. Bell, a talented black journalist who came to California in 1860, and Peter Anderson, leader in the California Colored Convention movement. Until publication of the *Appeal,* the only hint of black public opinion on the war and the election of Lincoln is the existence of a petition signed by several hundred black Californians requesting help to leave the United States. The petitioners declared that American blacks found little hope for their future in the nation. Whether this petition was a symbolic protest or expressed a genuine desire to emigrate will probably never be known.

If the *Appeal* accurately reflected California black opinion about the Civil War, then Afro-Americans in the state were in agreement with Frederick Douglass, the great black abolitionist leader in the East, who assumed that only good would result from the use of arms against the Confederacy. The *Appeal* kept up a running commentary on the desirability of black troops and quoted leading white supporters of this view. During these years California was not asked to send troops to the eastern war zones and was given the responsibility instead of manning the abandoned western forts and guarding the silver from Nevada. In 1863, the Union government even exempted California from the draft of that year.

However, there were California blacks who by 1863 wished to participate in the eastern military struggle. Efforts in this direction, while received politely in Washington, never resulted in the creation of California black companies. A few western blacks did enlist in black companies in the East through their own efforts, and some others enlisted in California companies which remained in the West. At least 26 black men in eight different companies were in uniform, all of them performing culinary duties.[9]

The first sign of enthusiasm for the war among California blacks occurred in April 1862 when Congress freed the blacks in Washington, D.C., by the method of compensated emancipation—paying the masters to free their slaves. Celebrations quickly followed in the San Francisco black community. Soon, while making it clear they felt that slavery itself still needed a frontal attack, blacks in their churches as well as in their public meetings raised funds to care for wounded Union soldiers. When the Emancipation Proclamation became a certainty, blacks dropped their cautious reserve towards the war. They had long observed the anniversary of the British Emancipation Act while doing little about July Fourth. But when the Emancipation Proclamation became a fact, grand events were promoted in the major black population centers. Even though they were not invited to participate in established July Fourth celebrations, they planned events of their own, stating clearly for the first time that they felt they were becoming an accepted part of the nation.

The Emancipation Proclamation evoked the most elaborate and joyous gathering of blacks yet seen in the city of San Francisco. Their support of the war accelerated from then on. The

Sanitary Fund, forerunner of the Red Cross, which was spear-headed by the Unitarian minister Thomas Starr King, benefited from Afro-American enthusiasm. King, who at all times after his arrival in California in 1860 showed friendship to the blacks, was grateful for the many hundreds of dollars they had raised for the Sanitary Fund. By 1864, enthusiasm for Lincoln had reached the point where San Francisco blacks, although still without the vote, held a mass meeting nominating him symbolically for a second term as President. By 1865, racism had ebbed sufficiently in San Francisco for the city's black community to be invited officially to participate in the Fourth of July parade. Afro-Americans in other California communities received mixed treatment in this regard.

In civil matters the Civil War period was an uneven story of gains and setbacks for California blacks. While racist attitudes were perhaps as strong as ever among the majority of white Californians, discrimination experienced a temporary decline and was somewhat muted during the years of civil combat. These were the years of the governorships of Leland Stanford (1862–1863), a Republican, and Frederic F. Low (1863–1867), a Unionist. In 1863, the onerous testimony law was finally democratized to the extent that at least blacks could testify with full equality. Indians and Chinese were still denied this benefit. Contemporary observers, both black and white, commented on the general economic well-being of blacks and the existence of some who were well-to-do. But problems remained in the area of education. From a few dozen the black population of children in the state had grown to hundreds, especially in San Francisco and Sacramento. As the number of children multiplied, blacks became interested in the vote as a way to improve their educational situation.

While there appeared to be no complaint about the fact that black teachers in California and even white teachers in black schools received less salary than white teachers in white schools, many blacks were concerned about good schools for their children. Contemporary descriptions leave little doubt that classrooms and facilities were inferior to the accommodations provided white children. Furthermore, high schools were virtually barred to black children. In the 1860s more and more black children came of high school age. San Francisco blacks valiantly worked to establish a private black high school, the Livingstone Institute, but this facility lasted only a decade. Though integration had opened many high schools to blacks, it was not until 1890, through the Wysinger case in Visalia, that the last vestiges of high school segregation ended.[10]

It was also in the 1860s that San Francisco blacks began the struggle to achieve equal access to the city's railways. During the Civil War two instances of ejection of black passengers, one a man and the other a woman, were successfully fought in the local courts with damage awards in each case. But these cases did not end discrimination by the city's lines. After the Civil War, the best-known case involved Mary Ellen (Mammy) Pleasants. She fought her grievance to the state Supreme Court, and won a damage award. As late as 1870, one of the city's lines again ejected a black woman passenger, but the railway lost the resulting suit for damages and shortly thereafter went bankrupt.

Though these cases had importance for Afro-Americans, their emotions were aroused most by the struggle over the right to vote. They raised that issue frequently in the pages of the *Appeal*. By 1865, at the time of the Fourth Colored Convention, public opinion had crystalized to the point of readiness. The convention took place in Sacramento in October and had the help of a second black weekly. Phillip Bell, having had a falling out with Peter Anderson, left the *Appeal* and began publishing the *Elevator*. Personalities rather than issues caused this split, and the dangers of an emotional confrontation at the convention threatened the movement. The two groups suspended their rivalry briefly that year to share publicly their common grief over the assassination of Abraham Lincoln.

The concerns of the fourth convention vividly reflected changing times. The first three conventions—in 1856, 1857, and 1858—had concerned themselves almost exclusively with the right of equal testimony in the courts of the state. In 1863, when this right had been won, it faded as an issue. National Afro-American leadership then began demanding that blacks be granted the right to vote. Emotion mounted rapidly, and by 1865 this demand had become the burning issue for blacks and much discussed among whites as well. At the convention in

Sacramento speech after speech urged the justice of the black man's claim to the franchise and its validity as a right based on his religion, his contributions to American life, and, more pointedly, his participation in the Union army. Other issues were also discussed. Education received more attention than at prior conventions, reflecting the growth of the black school-age population. Interest in the building of the transcontinental railroad was expressed by many delegates who called for the employment of 20,000 ex-slaves to work on its construction.

But the resolutions of the Fourth Colored Convention were not to be heard. The transcontinental railroad would be built by Chinese and Irish labor, and the demand of California's Afro-Americans for the right to vote was ignored by the 1865 California Union (Republican) state convention. Nonetheless, the blacks in San Francisco could feel that there was some good will still available to them in 1865. The city officially invited them for the first time to participate in the Fourth of July festivities. For them the blacks prepared lavishly and enthusiastically. In 1866, the invitation was not repeated because the political climate within that single year had moved to the right on racial issues. Henry H. Haight, a former Republican now turned Democrat, was elected governor. He was hostile to blacks as voters, and his followers in the state legislature shared his attitude. The lawmakers refused to give blacks (not to mention Indians and Chinese) the vote, and they had to wait until passage of the Fifteenth Amendment in 1870 for that right to be extended to them.

Black activities in southern California lagged behind those in the northern half during the first decades of statehood. Although many of the late eighteenth-century settlers of Los Angeles were of mixed ancestry, with the passage of time the importance of the African element in their ancestry lessened. The descendants of these settlers considered themselves Mexicans.[11] During the era of the gold rush individual blacks of United States origin worked and lived in widely scattered locations in the sparsely settled region south of the Tehachapis, with a handful residing in Los Angeles.

This small group of blacks, living in an environment dominated in the 1850s and 1860s by Americans from the southern states, produced some notable individuals. The best-known personality of those decades was Biddy Mason, an ex-slave who in 1855 battled her Mormon master for her freedom and gained it for herself, her family, and another family of slaves. The Mormons, who had settled in San Bernardino and then left en masse in 1858, had slaves with them who were given the option of remaining in California. Most of them remained and eventually entered the small Los Angeles community of free blacks. Biddy Mason, through hard work, became a property owner of some importance in Los Angeles, as did the black Owens family, into which members of the Mason family later married. Equally well known was a black barber and "character" named Peter Biggs. He gained much notoriety during the Civil War as a black who favored Jefferson Davis over Abraham Lincoln. However, during these early years, there were too few Afro-Americans in southern California to establish a significant community life, although Mason was reportedly holding religious services in her home for interested blacks. Life for black and white alike moved at a slow pace in the southern part of the state and reflected the pastoral setting. Blacks experienced a slow growth in numbers that accelerated sharply near the end of the century with a general increase of population in southern California.[12]

At the end of the first two decades of statehood, blacks remained few in number. They had laid foundations of association, however, and a few were business people in the northern cities of California, while many throughout the state were property owners. By far the greatest numbers were engaged in the service and food trades as productive members of the expanding society.

CHAPTER TWO

New Struggles in the Gilded Age

BETWEEN 1860 AND 1880, the black population in California increased, but that growth was small compared to the expansion of the white population. In 1860 and 1870 the number of blacks was about five thousand, although the official census (which invariably overlooked many blacks) placed the number closer to four thousand. The 1880 census gives a figure of 6,018. Most of these Americans were still of the gold rush generation, but there is evidence suggesting that more than a few ex-slaves migrated to California after the Civil War. While the Radical Reconstruction period, which began in 1867–68, fostered hope among blacks in the former slave states, the period also brought much turmoil and suffering. To escape their fate, some blacks made their way to California. The press gives a few clues about this small migration, especially in its occasional observations that cotton was being raised in the San Joaquin Valley and that ex-slaves were being brought out to do the work. Other brief notes refer to freedmen as members of the laboring force.[1] As of 1880, most blacks were still living in northern California. Los Angeles had only 188 Afro-Americans as compared to San Francisco's 1,628. Fast-growing Alameda County across the Bay had 686. All but two counties in 1880 recorded black residents, although the number remained small.

While the Democrat-controlled political climate in the state was either indifferent or hostile to black interests, national Re-

publican administrations were still sufficiently positive that
blacks felt encouraged to participate in civil rights activities. The
relative economic security of many blacks also served as an in-
ducement for such activities. Though Afro-Americans were still
heavily employed in the service and food trades, unemployment
was minimal. Some were active in gold mining, which had
shifted from panning to quartz mining, and had organized independent black mining companies. The ex-slave Mose Rodgers
gained the reputation of being an excellent hydraulic mining
superintendent whose operations in Mariposa County were
prosperous. He was typical of the former slave who did well and
then became a leader in the convention movement.[2]

In 1870, when California blacks finally won the vote through
the Fifteenth Amendment to the Constitution, they measured
their gains and decided to test the waters. High on their agenda
was an examination of the distressing state of education for their
children. Second-rate school facilities for black children, funded
by local government and paid in part by taxes levied on black
parents, irritated them. But they disliked the inequality of opportunity even more. It was clear that "separate" was never
"equal," and insistence on school integration generated a parallel
demand for proper funding. The law in 1871 provided for separate schools where there were ten or more black school-age
children and for the admission of these children if they were
fewer than ten and *if the local whites had no objection*.[3] Conse-
quently, black school children were left with no schools in many
rural areas. To remedy this situation a call was made for an
"Educational Convention" to take place in Stockton in November 1871.

The Educational Convention met at the church of Jeremiah B.
Sanderson, who was the most distinguished black pedagogue in
California. The delegates decided first to ask the legislature to
amend the state's educational code so as to halt the segregation
of black children. The Chinese were not included in their re-
quest because the delegates felt that such a broadening of the
campaign would ensure its defeat in the anti-Oriental atmosphere of nineteenth-century California. A champion for the
black cause was found in state Senator S. J. Finney of San Mateo
County who in 1871 introduced a bill to end segregation for

Tombstone of Louden Nelson in Evergreen Cemetery, Santa Cruz, California. (*Photo by Patricia T. Lapp.*)

Afro-American children. When the bill met defeat the next year, the executive committee of the Educational Convention turned to the courts for help.

During the summer of 1872, black leaders prepared for the court case by collecting money at many meetings, the most important of which took place in San Francisco, Sacramento, Stockton, and Marysville. (Contact at this time with the small Los Angeles black community did not seem to be worth the effort.) One of the most important achievements of the black organizers was their success in obtaining the services of a prominent lawyer, John W. Dwinelle, who had long held sympathies for black causes.

The grievance that explains this fresh surge of activity among blacks, especially those in San Francisco, can be understood from a description of the city's school facilities for black children which appeared on July 11, 1874, in the weekly Afro-American newspaper, the *Appeal*:

> There has been no improvement made in the condition of the main school on Russian Hill, which resembles a picture of Noah's Ark landed on Mount Ararat, and the other, a small room rented by the Board of Education, in a dwelling house in the neighborhood of Fifth and Folsom streets. There are 43 or more splendidly built school houses in the city suited or adapted to every neighborhood, while colored children have to travel the two extremes of the city to gratify the prejudices of proscription.

Not surprisingly, the first opportunity for a court case on the desegregation issue occurred in San Francisco. The attempts of Mary Frances Ward, a young black girl, to enter the Broadway School were denied by school principal Noah Flood on the grounds that there was a "colored" school that she could attend. So began *Ward* v. *Flood*, which went all the way to the state Supreme Court. Eighteen months later, in 1874, the court ruled that Mary Ward's rights had not been denied since there was an all-black school available to her. This was an early enunciation of the separate but equal doctrine, which the U.S. Supreme Court would approve in 1896 in *Plessy* v. *Ferguson*. In the *Ward* decision, however, there was a small gain. In school districts where there was no school for black children (the law required no separate school for blacks if they numbered fewer than ten), the community was compelled to let the black children enroll in the white school.[4] For the first time such children living in the rural and less populated regions of California were able to get an elementary education. The decision did not come too soon. A professional teachers' organization in the state estimated that in 1874 one-fourth of school-age black children were not in school.

Even before the *Ward* decision, segregation in education had begun to weaken. In 1872, Oakland's school system permitted black children to enter the elementary schools with white children, and there were no difficulties. By the last half of the 1870s school districts everywhere were closing their segregated schools and enrolling black children in white schools. This was often done over the protests of racist-minded newspapers and local pressure groups. In San Francisco the principal argument in favor of integration was not grounded in the demand for equality but rather the need to trim budgets and to operate the schools more economically. During the depression of the seventies this was a powerful argument even with prejudiced whites.

When the Fifteenth Amendment in 1870 gave the vote to all blacks in the United States who still did not have it, California's Afro-Americans entered the political process for the first time. Throughout the rest of the decade they remained, with only occasional waverings, in the camp of the Republican party. Any hesitations of loyalty occurred generally over issues that were close to California blacks on the local scene and only occasionally over national issues. With politics now open to them, blacks organized Republican clubs in communities where the talent was available. The largest of these clubs was in San Francisco where the hundreds of black voters could be the swing vote between the Republicans and the Democrats. But even where their votes were not of such significance, blacks still remained keenly interested in politics and joined Grant-Colfax clubs, Newton-Pacheco clubs, and even Charles Sumner clubs in a quixotic effort to promote the presidential candidacy of that Massachusetts Republican senator who was the blacks' greatest national civil rights champion in the early 1870s. Senator Sumner had introduced a national civil rights bill, and California blacks pinned their hopes on this measure to achieve school integration. The bill became law in 1875, but the provisions for integrated education had been deleted due to lack of support by Republicans. (The U.S. Supreme Court would find the bill unconstitutional in 1883.) Black loyalty to the regular Republicans is most evident in their rejection of the candidacy of the Republican bolter Horace Greeley, who had long been an opponent of slavery.

In spite of their loyalty, California's black Republicans had their moments of doubt about the party of Lincoln. They detected foot-dragging by state Republicans before 1870 when blacks felt California should grant them the vote by state law. They found Republicans in the state admonishing blacks not to

From the SAN FRANCISCO DAILY EXAMINER, Aug. '69

Shall Negroes and Chinamen Vote in California?

READ!

AN ADDRESS

BY THE

DEMOCRATIC STATE CENTRAL COMMITTEE

TO THE VOTERS OF CALIFORNIA.

"push too fast" in school matters, and they saw themselves getting next to nothing in the way of job appointments when Republicans had power to grant them. While most California blacks
remained true to the Republican party, they had no alternative
party to join. There was little in the Democratic party of the late
nineteenth century to attract them.

During the years when the Chinese issue and the railroad
issues wracked California politics, blacks supported the Republican view. The Chinese issue was particularly awkward for
them; on the one hand, they deeply resented the hostility to the
Chinese based on racist concepts, but on the other, they were
troubled by the big employers' (usually Republicans) prefer-
ence for Chinese labor. To counter this, the black press, in an
attempt to persuade employers to hire black labor, frequently
pointed to the fact that blacks were not only Americans, but
also Christians and English-speaking. At the same time the black
press was generally favorable to the railroad monopoly and the
restraint of union activity.

Without exception, the black press opposed the Irish-
dominated Workingman's party of the seventies. It also opposed
the 1879 state constitutional convention, which had the support
of the Workingman's party. Rivalry between the Afro-American
and Irish working-class communities had arisen out of job competition at the lowest rung of the labor ladder in the early decades of the nineteenth century. This hostility in New England
and New York then spread to the West Coast. The attitude of
blacks toward unions is easy to understand since the emergence
of unionism was so often associated with black exclusion from
jobs.[5]

The mood of this rivalry with the Irish must have reached
Sacramento, but did not enter the deliberations of the Fifth
State Colored Convention which assembled in November 1873.
The convention, however, gave evidence of other developments
in California's black communities. The number of delegates revealed that while San Francisco and Sacramento remained the
major centers of black life in the state, Stockton had moved
ahead of Marysville to number three in size, San Jose emerged
as a new center, and for the first time Los Angeles had represen-
tation. Also, an examination of the names of the delegates re-

veals the increased participation of ex-slaves, who had by now achieved relatively comfortable lives. Since *Ward* v. *Flood* was still pending before the state Supreme Court, the issue of education was very much on the minds of the delegates. The foot-dragging of the Republican party at the national level, where Senator Charles Sumner's civil rights bill was having trouble, plus the evasiveness of the California Republicans over the efforts at integrated education in the state, raised some criticism of the party among the delegates. Though a resolution publicly criticizing the party was turned aside, rumblings of discontent continued. In spite of uncertain political support from whites, however, the convention delegates decided to press for integrated education.

From this period to the end of the century, the growth of the black community was constant but slow, always hovering at one percent of the total population. The Chinese, Mexican, and Native American minority groups were still considerably larger. In 1880 the U.S. census reported 6,018 blacks in California, and in 1890, there were 11,322. In the major cities of the state blacks were still predominantly in the service, food, and menial occupations. However, a considerable number of businessmen could still be found in the larger urban centers, especially in San Francisco.

Little is known of the reasons for the slow growth of the California black population in the two decades immediately following the Civil War. A contemporary black westerner opined that many eastern blacks felt that it was dangerous to make the journey through unsettled country because of hostile Indians.[6] This impression of fear would be strong with eastern blacks because it was in the post–Civil War years that the all-black military units in the West were assigned to fighting Indians.

Basic research is scanty for the latter third of the century in western black history, but some facts are known. The near doubling of the state's black population by 1890 is explained by the real estate and land boom in southern California, which produced a black population gain in Los Angeles County from 188 in 1880 to 1,817 in 1890, a tenfold increase. In the same general area similar sharp increases took place. In 1880 the Fresno County black population was 40 and by 1890 it was 457. Even

Kern County went from 4 to 130 in that ten-year period. Southern California was fast catching up with the northern counties of the state.

The above statistics stand in contrast to the growth of the black communities in the northern part of the state. In San Francisco the increase in the black community was imperceptible, going from 1,628 in 1880 to 1,847 in 1890. The same was true for Alameda County across the Bay, where Oakland is located and where the figures were 686 in 1880 and 785 in 1890. In Sacramento County there was a small decline in the black population from 560 in 1880 to 513 in 1890. The number three and four counties in black population in the gold rush era, Yuba and San Joaquin, reflected different rates of growth between 1880 and 1890. In San Joaquin County, where there was some general growth of the white population, the black population, chiefly in Stockton, rose from 328 in 1880 to 353 in 1890. In Yuba County, where the white population suffered a slight decline, the black population, mainly in Marysville, dropped from 247 in 1880 to 218 ten years later. Whether this decline represented stability or stagnation for the black community in Marysville is unknown. Perhaps the latter, for Marysville's best-known black citizen, Edward Duplex, had by then moved his barber shop to Wheatland in the southern end of the county.

Throughout the state the census records of rural counties for 1880 and 1890 revealed a seesaw of small growths and small declines of the black population. In general terms, the northern counties of the state showed most of the declines, but there were surprising examples of growth in Santa Clara County, where the black population grew from 54 in 1880 to 221 a decade later. In the years after the gold rush there was a small but constant number of black farmers, farm tenants, farm workers, and cowboys (vaqueros) scattered throughout the state. In numbers, they were usually less than a hundred in spite of considerable exhortation by black leadership that more blacks should turn to agriculture. The still-fresh memory of slavery gave blacks a deep aversion to working on the land. Brief attempts at cotton raising by white promoters in southern California resulted in the rapid loss of their imported black labor shortly after arrival. These blacks usually headed for Los Angeles.

Why didn't Black people ?

Some general reasons can be cited for the growth of the black population in California. The coming of the railroads to the West was very important since many of the railroad workers, especially sleeping car porters and "red caps," were black men. Redcaps and Pullman porters were as familiar a sight to an older generation as airline stewardesses are to today's airline passengers. Many of these black railroad workers settled or retired with their families in western cities. They and other black migrants gradually introduced a new generation of western blacks who replaced the generation of gold-rush blacks who were now dead. In the 1880s and 1890s the older generation's two newspapers, the *Pacific Appeal* and the *Elevator,* ceased publication and were replaced by other ventures into black journalism.

Another reason for the rapid growth of the southern California black community in comparison with its northern counterpart was the greater expansion of trade unionism in the Bay area. The tragic practice in so many urban areas of newly unionized white workers excluding blacks created deep hostility to unions among blacks. This began early in the century in eastern cities and continued in California, especially among the craft unions. In the turn-of-the-century decades unionism made significant strides in San Francisco but was deterred in Los Angeles by powerful antiunion sentiment among employers led by Harrison Gray Otis, owner of the *Los Angeles Times.* Typical of the San Francisco story is the case of the Palace Hotel. When this luxury hotel opened in 1875, it was staffed by a full contingent of hundreds of trained black employees, many with previous experience in Chicago, in service and culinary categories. In the 1880s black workers at the Palace were sharply reduced, and by the first decade of the twentieth century black workers had been completely replaced by whites.[7] Blacks planning migration to California were often urged to avoid San Francisco and to go instead to Los Angeles, which was considered a "good town for colored folks."

Job discrimination in San Francisco drove Jamaica-born J. Alexander Somerville to southern California. Finding employment in Redlands, he saved enough money to enter dental school and graduated from the University of Southern California as the first black dentist in California. This was at the turn of the century, and Dr. Somerville was not allowed to forget his color. In his autobiography he noted that the press did not call him a Negro or a colored man when he graduated with highest honors, but referred to him as a "West Indian."[8] He also recalled that when he sought to open an office, landlords refused to rent to him. He finally opened an office in Los Angeles at Fourth and Broadway.

Discrimination and racist union pressures in San Francisco caused other blacks to move across the Bay to Oakland and to precipitate the sharp growth of the black community in Alameda County. By 1900 Oakland's black population had grown to over a thousand, most of this increase occurring in a decade when the state's total black population experienced no growth. During that same decade Los Angeles County's black population grew from 1,817 in 1890 to 2,841 in 1900. While the greater growth of the black population in the twentieth century would continue to be in the southern part of the state, Oakland kept pace with Los Angeles, and in 1920 both cities were the only ones in California where the black population was ten percent of the total.

Some of the reasons for the shifting black population can be found in national events. The years between 1890 and 1910 were bitter ones in the South, where most of the American black population still lived. The full consequences of the collapse of Radical Reconstruction in the 1870s began to take effect and full-scale "legal" disfranchisement and discrimination became the daily experience for blacks, sometimes accompanied by terror and lynching. Those who had the financial means sought better economic and educational opportunities elsewhere and escaped from open terror. This condition produced a steady trickle of Afro-Americans to the northern states. And some came west.

The small growth of the black population in California until the twentieth century will require further study. What migration there was apparently came from all regions of the country. Like the gold-rush generation of blacks, the newcomers may have been especially energetic and daring in undertaking the long trip to the West.

CHAPTER THREE

New Black Pride and Pressure Groups

CALIFORNIA'S BLACK POPULATION had nearly doubled by 1910, but it was between 1910 and 1920 that continued sharp growth revealed new vitalities in the black communities, especially in Los Angeles and the Bay Area. When William E. B. Du Bois, the famed Afro-American writer and first editor of *Crisis,* the official organ of the National Association for the Advancement of Colored People, visited California in 1913, he observed that

> Los Angeles is not Paradise, much as the sight of its lilies and roses might lead one at first to believe. The color line is there sharply drawn. Women have had difficulty in having gloves and shoes fitted at the stores, the hotels do not welcome colored people, the restaurants are not for all that hunger. . . . The new blood of California . . . has captured Los Angeles, but is just penetrating Oakland and San Francisco. In these latter cities the older easier-going colored man, born free . . . , still holds sway and looks with suspicion upon the Southern and Eastern newcomer. Then, too, the white trades unions have held the Negro out and down, so that here one finds a less hopeful, pushing attitude.[1]

In the decade of Du Bois's visit World War I occurred, bringing to California many more blacks seeking employment. In the same period black journalism showed new vigor, especially in southern California. The *Negro Year Book* for 1916–1917 reported nine black newspapers for the state. Five of them were in

A gathering of Afro-American motorcar owners in Los Angeles circa 1913. A prominent guest was W. E. B. Du Bois, standing fourth from the left.

Los Angeles and one in Bakersfield. Two were published in Oakland, reflecting the growing importance of that community in contrast to San Francisco, where there was evidently no longer a local black paper. The only other black newspaper was published in Sacramento.

Also in the decade of Du Bois's visit, two long-lived national black organizations—the National Association for the Advancement of Colored People (NAACP) and the Urban League—were born and soon chartered western branches. When the NAACP and the Urban League entered the California black scene before World War I, there were many with experience in leadership. Church and fraternal organizations had been a part of California black community life for decades. In the earlier years the African Methodist Episcopal churches were more pre-eminent, but, as time went by, the black Baptist churches came to share in this importance and, as the migrations from the South swelled at the turn of the century, the Baptists became the larger of the major denominations in California's black life. Also of importance in enriching the life of some middle-class blacks and providing leadership experience were the black Masonic lodges that had been a part of Afro-American life since the early days of the Republic. Under the inspiration of Booker T. Washington, Afro-American Leagues and National Negro Business Leagues were formed, and they had their California segments. These appeared to be most active between 1890 and 1910.

The NAACP was born in the East in 1909 as a result of the coming together of black and white liberals who were outraged at the racism so evident in the nation. These men and women were also a reflection of the Progressive era of reform that marked those pre–World War I years. The founding of the NAACP was practically the only evidence of concern about blacks in this era. The central black figure in this movement was the aforementioned William E. B. Du Bois.

Precisely when the first chapters of the NAACP were organized in California is not clear, but by 1913 one was in existence in Los Angeles. By 1915 there was also a chapter in northern California with its strongest base in Oakland. What made these two chapters especially visible was an event in the white world of the movie industry. In 1915 David Wark Griffith completed his artistically breathtaking and ideologically destructive film *Birth of a Nation,* originally called *The Clansman.* This film, with its path-breaking innovations, presented nearly three hours of distorted Civil War and Reconstruction history which made blacks into one-dimensional childlike fools, incompetents, brutes, or lechers. In San Francisco and Los Angeles the NAACP fought to have the film either not shown or censored. In San Francisco some offensive footage was cut, but not in Los Angeles, where the *California Eagle,* one of the earliest twentieth-century black newspapers, campaigned unsuccessfully for editing.[2]

Even so, life in California was attractive to many blacks. Frenzied real-estate competition reduced prices and assisted many Afro-Americans of modest income to become home-owners. This was particularly true in Los Angeles and Oakland, where the number of black homeowners was proudly reported from time to time in the national black press and where great numbers of blacks held jobs on the lower rungs of the civil service. In 1917, Oakland blacks, then estimated to number about five thousand, proudly published a *Colored Directory* with scores of pictures of their homes and churches. The introduction noted that the directory had grown from 76 pages in 1915 to 140 in 1917 and further observed that

> the colored man's property in Northern California certainly is more conspicuous today than ever before and clearly indicates possibilities that defy the most active human imagination to fully comprehend his final development.

The directory received the compliments of Booker T. Washington. Further evidence of the euphoria that possessed some Oakland blacks about living in California can be seen in the 1915 poem reproduced in this book, "I Love You, California."

In Los Angeles the police force hired the first blacks in the state. Considerable numbers also obtained jobs on the lower levels of the civil service. The attractions of southern California intensified. Especially was this true of the increasing number of blacks who now were coming from southwestern states. For them the lower-level salaries were high by comparison with their former incomes.

But the prospects for factory employment were also present.

SOUVENIR

Concert Extraordinary
OAKLAND, CAL., 1915

PROF. R. G JACKSON

I LOVE YOU, CALIFORNIA
F. B. SILVERWOOD

I love you, California; you're the greatest state of all'
I love you in the winter, summer, spring, and in the
fall,
I love your fertile valleys; your dear mountains I adore
I love your grand old ocean, and I love your rugged
shore.

CHORUS—*William Nauns Ricks*

You are welcome to dear California,
Professor Jackson, for your fame;
From the East to the West you are known as the best
That from old Kansas ever came.
There the noble John Brown sought our freedom,
Here we glory in his name.
So we welcome you more to the State we adore
To our dear old California.

I love your old gray Missions, love your vineyards
stretching far;
I love you California, with your Golden Gate ajar;
I love your purple sunsets, love your skies of azure
blue,
I love you, California, I just can't help loving you.

It should be remembered that Los Angeles was largely a non-union town. In 1926 Charles S. Johnson, a black sociologist at Fisk University, surveyed black employment in Los Angeles industry and found that out of 456 plants, at least 50 hired blacks at various levels of skill and income. He even observed black foremen supervising Mexican and Anglo workers. Johnson's study revealed that racial taboos were a job boon for some blacks in a department store. In this case management replaced white male "attendants" and elevator men with blacks in order to stop time-wasting flirtation and conversation between male employees and white sales girls.[3]

The image of California, at least southern California, as an attractive place for blacks was undoubtedly strengthened in 1928 when the first western convention of the NAACP took place in Los Angeles. This occurred with much fanfare and elaborate preparations well supported by the local NAACP chapters. State and local officials gave the event further stature by their presence and their welcoming speeches.

While blacks continued to migrate to California, once arrived they found the state something less than an interracial paradise. In the large cities there were hotels that would not receive them, restaurants that would not serve them, and innumerable public places, such as swimming pools and parks, that would segregate them. Even black and white nurses attending white patients in hospitals were required to eat in separate dining rooms. But the most glaring handicap developed in the 1920s with the use of real estate covenants to prevent the expansion of black communities into new areas. Gradually black residential areas turned into slums where overcrowding and other economic factors deteriorated the quality of life. The NAACP waged legal struggles to prevent discrimination and won a few victories. In the rural areas of the state the segregation of blacks was even more intense. The degree of racial prejudice among rural Californians, many of them originally from the South and poorly educated, was more pronounced than in the urban areas where there was some enlightened middle-class influence. In the small towns the segregated billiard hall was the most visible evidence of discrimination.

California became the setting for a turn-of-the-century attempt to create a self-sufficient black-controlled, all-black town. Similar attempts had already been made in Kansas and Oklahoma with varying degrees of success. In California a former army chaplain, Colonel Allen Allensworth, was the town organizer. Born a slave, he had escaped to freedom before the Civil War and, after some years, had entered the ministry. In time, he became a chaplain in the 24th Infantry (of "buffalo soldiers" fame). During the Spanish-American War he was still in this capacity and at its end he retired as lieutenant-colonel. He settled in California at a time when the fortunes of blacks in the South were at their lowest ebb. The rhetoric of white racism was raining heavy blows on the American black in an attempt to prove him incapable and inferior. Allensworth hoped to create in the state an all-black community which would be self-sufficient, a model of accomplishment, and a place where black people could live with dignity.

Allensworth chose an isolated site in Tulare County for his dream city, and by 1910 the first of several hundred settlers had arrived there. For about a decade the town of Allensworth struggled to survive as a viable community, but too many problems arose to challenge its future. The shortage of water was a chronic difficulty in this parched country and rail transportation was not readily available. Ironically, an additional obstacle to the development of Allensworth came from the blacks in Los Angeles who favored integration and not separateness. An Allensworth-supported proposal for an all-black state industrial school within the confines of the town had all the look of Jim Crow to the urbanized blacks of Los Angeles. This community, about to give birth to its first NAACP chapter, fought the industrial school idea and it died. Failing to achieve economic vitality, the town's small black population dwindled and the effort was given up. Allensworth may achieve a new importance as a monument, since it has been declared a state historical site and funds are being raised to restore it.[4]

Of considerable significance was the entry of California blacks into politics. In 1919 the first black state legislator arrived in Sacramento. He was Ohio-born Republican Frederick M. Roberts, a man with a teaching and journalism background. He edited and published *New Age,* a Los Angeles black newspaper. Assemblyman Roberts continued to represent his Los Angeles district until 1933. In these years professional black politicians were still attached to the party of Lincoln. With the exception of some elements of progressivism in the Democratic party of

New York, there was little to attract blacks to the Democratic party nationally. The southern and intensely racist wing of the party still dominated it and Congress in so many ways that most blacks in the United States saw only the hands of the lynch mob and the Ku Klux Klan in the Democratic party. Not until the era of Franklin Delano Roosevelt did that feeling change. But with the arrival of Frederick Roberts on the scene, there was the first evidence that blacks in California were preparing to shape western history and not be passively shaped by it. While Roberts's public career needs scholarly attention, it is known that he worked in the state Assembly to prevent racist materials from being used in the California schools.[5]

If significant political strength for blacks in the state was a long way off, economic strength also continued to lag in the 1920s. Blacks held only the barest grip on industrial employment in the state, and in the wide range of service and menial employment where blacks were numerous, this decade introduced a new competition. Many Japanese, Mexican, and Filipino immigrants were arriving in California to seek out jobs on the lower rungs of the economic ladder. Since the new arrivals were accustomed to standards of living much lower than those of black Americans, they were much in demand by employers of unskilled labor. Yet at the same time blacks continued to come to California and intensified the growing congestion, especially in a southern California area known as Watts. Increasingly, the new blacks of the 1920s came from the rural southwestern states and brought with them the usual unfamiliarity with urban living that marked all migrants from the farm to the city. Rural American white migrants had organizations like the YMCA and YWCA to guide them, and European immigrants had the famed settlement houses to prepare them for city life, but there were no similar provisions for American blacks. Into this void entered the Urban League. Even before World War I it was at work in the major urban centers of the East. By the 1920s the Urban League had recognized a need for its social service and job-seeking functions in California. Organizers were sent west and efforts were made in the Bay Area as well as in Los Angeles to found Urban Leagues. By the end of the 1920s one was beginning to function in Los Angeles where the ghettoization of the black community became ever more vivid.

A more short-lived black organization, which had begun on the East Coast during World War I, appeared in the 1920s in Los Angeles. This was the Universal Negro Improvement Association (UNIA), organized by a flamboyant and dynamic Jamaican black, Marcus Garvey. The organization's appearance in California marked the first evidence of black nationalism on the West Coast. In Los Angeles it vied with the more conservative NAACP and at least once, during and after a dramatic western visit by Marcus Garvey, was the larger organization. The UNIA rejected integration and the civil rights struggles, which characterized the work of the NAACP, but the competition for supporters did not reach the intensity of the hostility found in eastern cities. This manifestation of black nationalism passed from the western stage not to surface again until forty years later in the 1960s when it rose in new and more strident forms.

One cannot leave the decade of the 1920s without considering the enormous growth of the motion picture industry in Hollywood and its impact on blacks. Many historians of the film industry give 1915 as the year in which California filmmaking developed into a serious art form. In that year the remarkable but intensely antiblack *Birth of a Nation* was presented to the public by its brilliant southern-born director-producer, David Wark Griffith. It was produced in southern California where real blacks were employed to play in mob scenes and to portray menials. Leading black roles were played by whites in blackface.

As already noted, many blacks joined with the NAACP in picketing and protesting this film in California as well as in the rest of the country. But some blacks went into the movie-making business to combat the *Birth of a Nation* image of Afro-Americans. Most of these efforts took place in the East but one valiant effort occurred in Los Angeles. In 1915 the Lincoln Motion Picture Company, organized by George and Noble Johnson, produced motion pictures in the heart of the Los Angeles black community. For six years they struggled to produce films about black life with black actors. In 1921 their effort expired, the victim of a variety of factors, including uneven support from the black community, total neglect from the white film world, and constant financial and booking problems.[6]

In the white movie world blacks played buffoon, musical, or

menial roles until well after the end of World War II. But the revulsion against Hitler's racial theories had evoked a change of mood in Hollywood circles, and in the growing anti-Fascist temper of the industry blacks appeared in films of social commentary. Motion pictures began to hint at more than the discrimination faced by blacks in American life. This development was accompanied by a sharp rise in the employment of blacks as actors in the industry. The trend came to an abrupt end during the immediate postwar years as a consequence of the Cold War and the Red-hunt era that accompanied it. Black employment in films was the innocent victim of the witch hunt in Hollywood conducted by the House Committee on Un-American Activities. The jailings and blacklistings that resulted drove from Hollywood many writers who produced the kinds of scripts that give employment to black actors. Such scripts, because they dealt with social problems, were perceived as subversive by the House committee. For about a decade blacks found little employment in the film industry in roles other than menials. In 1963 a reversal began with the Oscar-winning performance of Sidney Poitier in *Lilies of the Field.* From then on the employment of black actors of both sexes experienced a remarkable rise.

In non-acting professions in Hollywood blacks were seldom in evidence. The motion picture industry's hiring practices were part of the explanation, but the preferences of blacks played a part as well. An article in *Crisis,* the NAACP magazine, reported in February 1946 that "on the whole Negroes have not concerned themselves . . . with the less glamorous phases of moviemaking and have concentrated specifically on acting."[7] In the more than thirty years since that report, the number of non-acting black professionals in filmmaking has increased sharply as a result of job opportunities in television as well as the movies. The filmmaking departments of the colleges and universities in California attest to the rise in interest by black students in this glamorous occupation.

Blacks after 1910 experienced some progress finding positions as they struggled for equality with the whites. Such organizations as the Urban League and the NAACP brought unity to their actions and helped them secure white-collar jobs and professional positions.

CHAPTER FOUR

Depression
and War

T HE GREAT DEPRESSION of the 1930s paradoxically
stimulated one of the largest migrations of southern
blacks to California. This depression decade saw only slightly
fewer blacks come to California than had come in the more
prosperous 1920s. Of course, this was also a period marked by a
surprisingly large migration to the West of whites from the
Middle West who came to escape the dust storms.

A glance at the *California Eagle,* the major Negro newspaper
in Los Angeles during the depression, would make the migration of blacks during these years seem even more astonishing.
Its pages were full of stories about police brutality, job discrimination, and segregation. An historian of the period, who
interviewed many of the migrants, found that letters from friends
and relatives were the major reasons the newcomers set out for
the Los Angeles area.[1] They evidently did not see copies of the
California Eagle before they arrived in the West.

Even with this unusual migration of blacks, the overall general migration westward was so enormous that in 1940 blacks
still were barely two percent of the total California population.
Though the entire state received additions to its population, the
larger part went to the southern cities of the state. Over 24,000
blacks settled in Los Angeles, and of the four cities other than
Los Angeles that got more than a thousand new black residents
in this decade, San Diego led the way. Fresno was also one of

these four, while San Francisco and Berkeley were the other two.[2]

The attraction that California, especially southern California, had for blacks in this hungry decade was a blend of fact and expectation. While the wave of unemployment that struck the country lagged before it reached California, it swept over the state in the early 1930s, and blacks had the highest unemployment rate of any group in Los Angeles. In addition, they had the lowest-paying jobs in the state, and organized labor prevented them from getting a serious foothold in industrial employment, although before World War II the state did not have much heavy industry. On the brighter side, blacks owned more homes in southern California than elsewhere and enjoyed income from low-paying jobs in Los Angeles that was higher than in the rest of the country. Furthermore, like most whites, blacks enjoyed California's mild weather and accepted easily the burden of unemployment where the sun shone regularly and where aid was available. Of great significance, too, were the beginnings of the vast national relief program that was provided by the Franklin D. Roosevelt administration. Many blacks in California were easily eligible for the benefits of these programs, and this very quickly had political consequences.

Black Republican Frederick M. Roberts had represented a Los Angeles Assembly district ever since 1919, but in 1934 he was challenged by a black Democrat, Augustus F. Hawkins, who waged a strong campaign. Hawkins defeated Roberts and thus signaled the California phase of the shift taking place nationally as blacks switched their allegiance from the Republican party to the Democrats. Hawkins, born in 1907 in Louisiana, came with his family to Los Angeles when he was ten years old. His father, although a successful pharmacist, had become disgusted with living in the South. In 1931 the young Hawkins received his degree in economics from UCLA, after which he entered the real estate business. In 1934 he was swept up by the excitement and idealism of Upton Sinclair's E.P.I.C. campaign. While Sinclair's political career in the Democratic party was brief and meteoric, Hawkins continued much less spectacularly as an elected official, but one who was returned to office year after year.

The 1934 gubernatorial election was the most unusual in

California history because of the emotion aroused in the electorate. Sinclair was an anti-Communist Socialist best known for his enormous volume of writing on social issues and the plans he intended to implement if he were elected governor. There was some black support for Sinclair, but how much is not clear. An official of the black Dining Car Cooks and Waiters Union organized Sinclair support clubs in Los Angeles and Oakland. Other blacks offered their personal backing. The anti-Sinclair forces drenched the black communities with statements about Sinclair's views on organized religion. These attacks clearly influenced many California voters. An anti-Sinclair film clip shown throughout California falsely purported to be a newsreel interview with a black minister who said that he was voting for Sinclair's opponent, Republican Frank Merriam, because the local minister wanted to "save his church." The black "minister" was a local prize fighter who also preached. Much bitterness resulted from this kind of electioneering, but the vote was nonetheless surprisingly close. Fortunately for Hawkins, he was able to sidestep the hostility, but he remained the only black elected official in California. Not until 1948 would conditions mature for the election of a second black state assemblyman, Byron Rumford of Berkeley, and he would also be a Democrat.

The red-baiting of Upton Sinclair raises the question of the extent of communism's appeal to blacks in California. The record suggests that it was minimal. Marxism had magic for a relatively small number. There were a few black Socialists before World War I. Nearly two decades later, during the Great Depression, some California blacks found the Communist party appealing because it was the only political party to defend blacks. Some blacks worked with the Communist party in the National Negro Congress, which became a party front organization, but this relationship was not of long duration. The slight Communist penetration of the NAACP was driven out by the NAACP leadership.[3] The masses of blacks in the thirties and forties, while rarely hostile to Communists, were passive to their Marxism and remained overwhelmingly in the world of conventional ideologies.

Depression-era California was also publicized by John Steinbeck's *Grapes of Wrath,* both as a novel and a film, which depicted the agricultural and migrant farm laborer. The film was a nearly all-white story and properly so. Afro-Americans in the turbulence of the migrant farm struggle were few in number because California blacks were mainly urban people. Even when they came from rural regions, they tended to be from small towns and villages.

In 1939 when the Second World War broke out in Europe, the consequences for California were immediate. American defense spending sharply accelerated, and on the West Coast shipbuilding and aircraft production boomed. During 1941 migration to California rose sharply over the previous three years, and blacks were part of this influx. Again, southern California received the lion's share of these newcomers. More than half of the 12,000 black migrants in 1940 went to Los Angeles, and the rest in varying numbers chose Long Beach and San Diego. Oakland, San Francisco, and Sacramento received most of the migrants to northern California. A much larger proportion of blacks than ever before came from the deep South and the Southwest. Word of job opportunities reached blacks in many ways. Most effective were the notices of job openings in the shipbuilding industries that went out through the thousands of state employment offices in every state in the nation. This writer remembers seeing such notices in a small town in Illinois in 1942 referring to such exotic locations as Mare Island and Hunter's Point. Identical notices were being read in Alabama, Louisiana, and Texas. For blacks this was a great opportunity to escape the low wage scales in the South. Until 1942, however, defense jobs elsewhere in the nation drew many more blacks than did those in California.

Even so, blacks experienced much opposition on racial grounds from employers until late 1942. Before that time employer indifference or discrimination, compounded by union restrictions, held down the number of jobs available to blacks. During this period of declining unemployment the percentage of blacks on relief steadily increased. Not until the dramatic threat in 1941 by A. Philip Randolph, the black president of the Sleeping Car Porters Union, of a protest march on Washington did President Franklin D. Roosevelt issue Executive Order 8802. This order required defense training programs to end discrimination and inserted a nondiscrimination clause into government defense contracts. It also set up a Committee on Fair Employment Practices. Armed with federal authority and support, blacks exerted pressure for the first time upon employers to open up jobs for them in the defense industry. Employers and unions now began to unbend. It should be said that some employers and unions had hired blacks even before this pressure. From the time of its founding in the 1930s, the CIO had been actively opposed to discrimination. On the West Coast, the most conspicuous example of such opposition was in the International Longshoremen and Warehousemen's Union, headed by Harry Bridges. However, an additional factor breaking down discrimination during these war years was simply the enormous growth of the aircraft industry in southern California, the shipbuilding and maintenance industry in the Bay Area, and the resulting labor shortages.[4]

Labor shortages on the West Coast were accentuated in the early days of the war by the evacuation of the Japanese. A too easily forgotten aspect of this evacuation is the story of black relations with the Japanese. Their association for years was amiable, and many blacks worked for Japanese employers in Los Angeles. Most Los Angeles Japanese lived in an area called "Little Tokyo." When they were evacuated, blacks—who were increasing in number during the war years—moved into the area en masse. (The same thing happened in the Japanese area of San Francisco.) There evidently were numerous intermarriages, because a considerable number of blacks visited daily with their spouses at the Los Angeles evacuation center. An ironic story in the Japanese-Negro relationship is reported by Roi Ottley, a black journalist. Japanese developers, he noted, had obtained a tract of Los Angeles land for home development some years before World War II and then found their efforts blocked by nearby whites on racial grounds. The Japanese developers rallied black support in a struggle against racism. The Japanese developers won and were allowed to proceed, but the new development was subsequently restricted against black occupancy.[5]

World War II was marked by much racial turbulence in the armed forces as well as among urban laborers. Segregation was still the rule in the armed forces during most of this war period.

One of the most dramatic events occurred in California in 1944 at a U.S. Navy loading station in Port Chicago, where black sailors loading shells were caught in a terrible explosion that killed hundreds. The men were stationed at nearby Mare Island and, not long after the tragedy, received orders to start loading again. This resulted in a mutiny in which fifty black sailors refused to obey the order. A court case ensued in which the local NAACP chapter, with help from its national office, fought unsuccessfully to free the mutineers. The explosion and trial were memorialized in the poem "Black Boat" by the prominent white California poet Julia Cooley Altrocchi, later published in her anthology *Girl with Ocelot and Other Poems* (Boston, 1964). After nearly two years and into the peacetime period, nearly all the men were freed through reduced sentences.

This wartime decade was one in which the West experienced its greatest influx of people in general and black people in particular. California received most of this migration. The Afro-American population in California went from 124,306 in 1940 to 462,172 by 1950. And again, the largest numbers of these arrivals went to the southern half of the state. Most of these newcomers, both white and black, came from southern and rural regions where educational opportunities were limited and where blacks enjoyed even fewer opportunities than whites. Black expectations, even allowing for the habit of lower expectations acquired in the southern environment, would inevitably rise in this new climate of democratic rhetoric and in the postwar world of the Four Freedoms. In several of the larger cities of the state interracial councils of civic unity and commissions on human relations were organized that gave heart to black aspirations. But powerful factors in the new environment acted as bars and deterrents to the hope of an early upward mobility.

As the last hired, many blacks were the first fired in the readjustment period of postwar industry. Not long after the war's end, blacks were conspicuously numerous on the unemployment compensation lines. When those funds were exhausted, their numbers began to rise again in the relief roles. However, not all blacks who were new to heavy industry were being laid off. A good number retained their jobs into the postwar boom, but they also faced a return of discriminatory practices. In the clerical and white collar areas of the private sector blacks were still very few in number. The breakthrough there would have to wait until the 1960s.

Illustrative of the change in working conditions from war to peace is the story told by sociologist C. Wilson Record about the young black Willie Stokes. Record follows Stokes from his life on a cotton farm in Mississippi in 1941 through his wartime experiences as a welder in the Kaiser shipyards in Richmond, California, where he received $10 for an eight-hour day. In 1946, when the war was over, Stokes was laid off, and then found work in a chemical plant near Richmond for $6.40 for an eight-hour day. He purchased his groceries in the same stores that he had patronized during the war, but the prices were now much higher. Not only was he no longer able to live on his wages, he had married and his family had grown larger. He was forced to cash in his war bonds to make ends meet. By 1947 Willie Stokes was unemployed and surviving on unemployment compensation. This aid was of short duration and soon the family was on county relief.[6]

For the mass of new black Californians the quality of life was also held back by the intensified real-estate practice of preventing the expanded black population from moving into new and better areas. Black residential areas gradually became ghettos and, in some cases, slums as congestion worsened. The restrictive covenant became an increasing irritant to black pride and especially to those blacks who by this time had the income to afford better homes in better neighborhoods. On the basis of the swelling numbers of blacks in California, a professional and business class of blacks was now in existence, and they were among the first to feel the stinging insult of the refusal by realtors to sell middle-class homes to them.

The legality of restrictive covenants was widely accepted before World War I. This practice persisted and intensified, keeping upward mobile minorities from improving the quality of their lives until the end of World War II. In 1947, concerned lawyers joined forces with the NAACP to put the issue before the United States Supreme Court, where in 1948 the restrictive covenant was struck down.[7] However, the decision was not strong enough to prevent discrimination in the selling and renting of homes from continuing under "private understanding" subterfuges. Nearly two decades would have to pass before the attack on housing discrimination would reach more intensive and successful levels. A few legal skirmishes in middle-class neighborhoods conducted by the NAACP in the Los Angeles area were won a few years before the 1948 Supreme Court decision, but the major housing struggles were yet to come. In the immediate postwar years legal battles over discrimination in public eating places were fought and won in the Los Angeles area. The *Negro Handbook* for 1949 reported three such victories where the courts awarded damages to black complainants.

In areas other than housing and restaurants, black professionals found themselves facing racial prejudice. In 1945, one month before the United Nations was born in San Francisco, the Los Angeles Bar Association, an all-white organization, found itself perplexed when a black attorney was put up for membership. In following traditional policy, the association took the stand that "the policy of the Association expressed in its constitution and in its past history is such that in the absence of a mandate from the membership to the contrary it has no other course than to deny members of the Negro race membership in the Association." Several association referenda and five years later, in 1950, the Los Angeles Bar Association gave black attorneys the right to membership.[8] A 1945 study of intercultural education in California found that black social workers were often denied membership in country professional organizations.

Such problems besetting a now much larger black population were soon to have their political and social consequences in an era of rising expectations of minority groups.

From Civil Rights to Black Revolt

I N 1954 A SIGNAL for action came across the country from the national capital. The Supreme Court of the United States, as the result of a case initiated by the NAACP, handed down the now famous decision in *Brown* v. *Topeka Board of Education,* which declared that separate was not equal. While this signal was directed to offending state and local governments in matters of education, it became in time a catalytic agent for a national protest movement that embraced the resentments of black people. This movement, or more accurately movements, began in the East and Middle West and then quickly spread across the country as the Civil Rights Movement. Its beginnings can be traced to 1942 in Chicago. Inspired by the principles of nonviolence espoused by Mahatma Gandhi, a group of blacks and whites came together to form the Committee of Racial Equality, soon to be called simply CORE. During World War II they successfully ended discriminatory practices in Chicago's restaurants in the downtown area. In the postwar period CORE had its ups and downs in similar efforts in the South while gradually gaining a national reputation as a pacifist-type civil rights organization. These young activists received frequent legal aid from America's oldest civil rights organization, the National Association for the Advancement of Colored People.

In 1961, five years after the *Brown* decision of the Supreme Court, CORE once again was in the forefront of the nonviolent civil rights struggle. In that year CORE initiated what became known as the "Freedom Ride." This Freedom Ride sought the integration of terminals and waiting rooms everywhere in the South. The nation watched as black and white young men endured the terror and beatings of racist whites all along their route. When it was over, CORE was a national household word. It resulted in the revival of moribund chapters of the organization and the founding of new ones. By 1963 there were CORE chapters in several major cities in California and they were girding for action.

The civil rights revolution that began in Montgomery, Alabama, in 1955 under the leadership of the Reverend Martin Luther King, gradually spread north and west until it reached California in 1963 under the leadership of CORE. The young people of CORE were supported by other black and white organizations and especially by the NAACP, which was compelled by the times to add street work to its activities in addition to the court actions that in the past had been its most common arena for accomplishment. In 1963 CORE members went into the Los Angeles streets to protest housing discrimination and de facto segregation in the schools. Their tactics were nonviolent although they broke the peace.

CORE's struggle to end housing discrimination in southern California focused on Monterey Park, where a black physicist had been denied a home. After five weeks of agitation the venture ended successfully. CORE then joined with the NAACP in an attempt to break down housing barriers for middle-class blacks, but further conclusive victories eluded them. After the arrest of some demonstrators, a thousand people joined forces on a Saturday in the summer of 1963 and marched to a suburban subdivision of Los Angeles. In spite of this activity and support by the state attorney general, who issued an injunction against one builder, the result was inconclusive. Some relief in the unbearable congestion in black communities was achieved, but de facto segregation continued.

In San Francisco the work of CORE and its allies took on more dramatic forms. The movement was concerned about jobs, and

[handwritten: note prior on data collection on hiring practices —]

in 1963 began picketing a restaurant chain called Mel's Drive-In to bring pressure for the hiring of blacks. This protest was followed the next year by an effort to get supermarkets to hire *[handwritten: Lucky]* blacks. Shopping carts would be filled to overflowing with food, including frozen food items, taken to the front of the stores, and abandoned near the cash register. In that same year, 1964, San Francisco CORE engaged in its most spectacular venture at gaining jobs for blacks. It took on the elegant Sheraton-Palace *[handwritten: I was arrested at both places]* Hotel and the extensive auto row on Van Ness Avenue. In both cases hundreds of young people sat down in these establishments until some commitment was made to hire blacks and, in some instances, they demanded that hiring go beyond just placing token blacks on the payroll. These actions made front-page national news, especially the photos showing the police arresting and dragging out the demonstrators.[1]

While these events were high points in CORE's work, the movement also engaged the corporate structure when it went after Bank of America in San Francisco and demanded that blacks be employed in the then lily-white world of banking. Today's young people who see minorities working as tellers in banks little realize that once it was not so. The immediate result of this dramatic movement by young blacks and their white allies was a ripple of tokenism in hiring in many occupational areas, including the crafts and building trades, where blacks were still few in number.

The year 1963 was a milestone in the civil rights movement nationally. The highly visible March on Washington took place that year, an action that was a coalition of many organizations and brought to the national capital a quarter of a million blacks and whites. Here Martin Luther King made his now immortal "I Have a Dream" speech. The national attention was captured by these events. By this time the brutalities of southern life had become common knowledge to most Americans who watched on television the heavy hand of southern law enforcement officers towards civil rights workers. Many young people, especially students, black and white, were caught up in the enthusiasm of the movement. But the civil rights revolution was soon overshadowed by the Black Revolution, which dramatically manifested itself in California.

For many blacks, whether in or out of the civil rights movement, life did not change much during the period between the
end of World War II and the beginning of the 1960s. In California, the problems of decent housing, jobs (especially for
youth), and police brutality were still chronic. The continued
migration of blacks to California intensified the population den-
sity of black communities and made them truly ghettos. Young
blacks grew up separated from the larger white world and their
own world became one of de facto segregation with declining
educational advantages. In this decade of rising expectations, a
long-muted sense of urgency came to the fore, especially among
black youth who, in typical American fashion, demanded hurried satisfaction. A less typical ingredient, however, was their
radical rhetoric. Even before the March on Washington, a black
student movement emerged on southern campuses that became
allied for a time with Martin Luther King's Southern Christian
Leadership Conference. It was called the Student Non-Violent
Coordinating Committee (SNCC). Early in the 1960s SNCC
moved in a radical direction, rapidly shedding its pacifist image
and gradually developing a generally antiwhite posture. In 1966
SNCC's best-known spokesman, Stokely Carmichael, uttered
for the first time the slogan "Black Power." This slogan was to
have an electrifying effect on the masses of black youth around
the country, especially in the urban centers. SNCC's radicalism
was shared by CORE, which began manifesting the same militant
posture and rhetoric. An illustration of the new mood was the
contemptuous rejection of the word "Negro" and the demand
that only "black" be used to refer to Afro-Americans.

The new mood introduced another new phrase, "black nationalism." What is now clear in retrospect is that black power
and black nationalism meant different things to different blacks.
This is well illustrated by what happened in California beginning
in the 1950s.

The Black Muslims, who were not in the mainstream of black
nationalism, were a thoroughly separatist and nationalist religious group which had adopted the religion of the Arab world.
They achieved a reputation for puritanical living and were gaining converts, to the astonishment of many, among black prison
inmates. Much of their success was due to the charismatic figure

of Malcolm X, who had himself once been a convict. It was probably Malcolm X's influence that explains Eldridge Cleaver's temporary conversion, which occurred while Cleaver was in jail. The Muslims, who had midwestern origins, grew rapidly in number in Los Angeles and San Francisco after World War II. They believed in economic self-sufficiency and ignored the political arena. Under their leadership many Muslim-owned small businesses were initiated and thrived in urban centers in California.

The main strength of the Muslims lay in the young black post–World War II migrants who faced the new frustrations of northern life. Older California blacks remained attached to their Christian black churches and generally ignored the Muslims. In the postwar years Malcolm X was highly successful in appealing to young blacks in and out of the Muslim movement. The vividness of his antiwhite oratory and call for blacks to separate from *(changed later)* whites in their struggles for black security and dignity profoundly influenced the membership of both CORE and SNCC. In the California chapters of these two organizations, as in the chapters elsewhere in the nation, the pressures led to memberships that were exclusively black. In deep disappointment and in some cases anger, radical and liberal whites left SNCC and CORE. *(not always — sometimes undeterred)* The older black organizations lamented this development with its antiwhite rhetoric only to earn the caustic criticism of the younger groups.

On the campuses of California's many colleges and high schools a phase of this nationalist movement appeared among the now considerable number of blacks attending school in the 1960s. This aspect of nationalism took the form of Black Student Unions (BSUs). Throughout California, and especially on campuses in or near large black communities, BSU chapters became springboards for a variety of campaigns. The most common scholastic demand was for a Black Studies program and a Black Studies Department controlled by blacks and taught by blacks. The rationale for such a program, which had genuine merit and was not seriously questioned by administrations, was the incontrovertible fact that the American black and his part in American history had often been omitted from American education. But questions also arose over who would teach these courses and who would hire the teachers, and would teachers have to be black. What complicated the problem from campus to campus in California, as well as elsewhere in the nation, was the fact that few academics had specific preparation to teach such courses. While southern black colleges had been offering Afro-American courses for decades and had talent enough for their own purposes, they were unable suddenly to provide teachers for the whole nation.

The result of this black studies campaign was the mushrooming all over the state in the 1960s of black studies programs of wide variation in quality and style. This development was accompanied by much struggle and grief over the issue of control and hiring of staff, a power that administrations were reluctant to surrender. This was a power demanded by the most militant and nationalist blacks, who believed it was essential to their struggle for "the control of their destinies."

The results of this struggle are still obscured by controversy and contradictory opinion. So many of the leading figures, black and white, have left the stage of this drama (according to Robert Brustein of Yale University, much of this movement had the quality of theater)[2] that collective assessments are hard to find. Tentative observations suggest that at the best-known institutions of higher learning the tone of the black studies programs was set by the most militant blacks and this repelled some of the black scholars. White scholars of black history were rarely encouraged to teach in these programs.

A classic case of confrontation occurred at San Francisco State University (then college) in 1968. The Black Student Union presented the administration with ten non-negotiable demands which essentially required complete control of every aspect of the black studies program by blacks. For the administration this demand was an unprecedented experience, but when the smoke cleared the BSU had gotten most of what it wanted. The administration retained the power of granting tenure to faculty in the black studies division. This power was apparently retained by most school administrations in California. With the passage of time it appears that this contributed to a constant turnover in black studies faculty. During the early and hurried years of these programs some of the teachers were persons of minimal qualifications who obtained positions because they were highly visible in the rhetorical aspects of the struggle.

By the end of the 1960s, there were black studies offerings in most institutions of higher learning and in many high schools. On this issue the Black Student Unions attained a degree of success in their confrontations with white-controlled administrations. Some of these administrators were ready to see the logic of black studies while others were frightened enough to grant such demands. Many blacks and some white teachers of American history became instructors in black history courses. The demand at all levels for black studies programs came with such speed and force, as far as school administrations were concerned, that the graduate schools were caught unprepared.

In southern California the control of the black studies program became a power struggle at UCLA between two noncampus groups of black nationalists, the "US" led by Ron Karenga, then a cultural black nationalist, and the Black Panthers, who were political nationalists. The cultural black nationalists believed that the strength-giving ingredient for Afro-Americans was a strong identification with African culture. Therefore, they felt American history and politics to be a waste of time. The political nationalists believed in gaining control of all aspects of black life, including political, educational, and economic institutions, especially those controlled by whites in black communities. In 1969, these two views and their respective organizations clashed on the UCLA campus and murders resulted. Many serious charges have been made; not least is the current charge that the FBI was aware of these hates and manipulated them to achieve the murders. The U.S. Senate Select Committee on Intelligence revealed FBI files which showed that the FBI encouraged the battle between "US" and the Panthers by fabricating insulting cartoons of the Panthers presumably done by "US" and also by sending provocative anonymous letters to leaders of both groups designed to stimulate trouble between them.[3]

Attention must be given to that wing of black thought which saw black power as a movement within the system to gain advantages similar to those achieved by twentieth-century white immigrants and their descendants. The unconventional wing of the movement to gain community status equal to whites was the Black Panthers.

The brand of political nationalism represented by the Black Panthers was born in Oakland, California, in 1966. Its founders, Huey Newton and Bobby Seale, were young men who had spent their teenage, formative years in post–World War II Oakland when that city's black population was growing faster than the local institutions and economy could absorb it. The city's police force found it especially difficult to adjust to the large number of black migrants. Young blacks, in turn, felt particularly harassed by the Oakland police. In this setting the Black Panther party flourished. Radical in style and rhetoric, it called itself Marxist-Leninist. It published a weekly paper which carried local as well as national news, and in its first half-dozen years employed language and illustrations that left little doubt about the organization's deep hatred for the police. The drawings of the smoking end of a gun and a pig's head on a uniform were virtually the paper's trademark. The organization rapidly caught the imagination of inner-city young blacks and spread eastward to the Atlantic Coast.

Police confrontations quickly became the mark of Panther activity, and newspaper reportage tended to obscure the fact that in most inner cities the police did not treat minority citizens with the deference with which they treated white citizens. The effect was a deep hatred of police by most blacks, and especially young blacks. The Panthers made popular the word "pig" as a substitute for the word "police" among blacks and white radicals. It was after bloody encounters with the police and the exposure in the 1970s of the FBI's attempts to destroy the Panther leadership that the Panthers moved into mainstream politics. The rhetoric softened, the guns became less visible, the *Black Panther* newspaper illustrations switched from smoking guns to pictures of black mothers, and in Oakland the Panther organization ran candidates for office and conducted free food centers. The organization's present direction is not clear, since its members are concerned with a variety of issues, and the remaining major leader, Huey Newton, is facing court trials.

Conventional black politics, though less colorful, consisted primarily of black Democrats pressing for black candidates in California elections. After being in the state Assembly for eight years, Augustus Hawkins was joined in that body in 1948 by a second black, William Byron Rumford, from the Berkeley-Oakland area. In 1962, two more were elected from the Los Angeles area, F. Douglass Ferrell and Mervyn Dymally. In 1964 San Francisco elected Willie L. Brown, Jr., to the state Assembly. (It is worth noting that the two black assemblymen from the Bay Area needed and received white votes to be elected.) In 1966 three more blacks were elected to the state Assembly from the Los Angeles area and one more from the Bay Area: Yvonne Brathwaite Burke, Bill Green, and Leon Ralph from Los Angeles, and John Miller from Berkeley. This period of major entry into mainstream politics also saw Hawkins leave the Assembly after the 1962 elections to take his seat in the House of Representatives in Washington as the first black congressman from the West.

Mention of Assemblyman Byron Rumford recalls one of California's most controversial political campaigns, waged around a piece of housing legislation of which he was the author and which bears his name. While previous legislation in the state had attempted to eliminate discrimination in housing, it had left prosecution of violations to the expensive court process. For minority peoples of color this was too often a burden they could not carry. The Rumford proposal provided for the presentation of grievances to the State Fair Employment Practices Commission, a procedure much more within the reach of the poor. The Rumford bill became law in 1963 and the realtors of California immediately prepared to overturn it by an initiative that was known as Proposition 14. It was the hottest issue in the election campaign of 1964 in California. Its proponents claimed that the main issue was the right of citizens to do what they wished with their property in the matter of selling or renting. Its opponents claimed that race prejudice and the rights of minorities to move where they pleased were the issues. In the fall elections, Proposition 14 won overwhelmingly and the Rumford Act was invalidated. Blacks and others read the returns as a naked manifestation of racism in California. However, a few years later Proposition 14 was overturned by the State Supreme Court (in *Reitman et al.* v. *Lincoln W. Mulkey*) and the Rumford Act was again in effect.

The consequences of this popular vote may never be com-

pletely known, though there were at least two significant events
that might have been triggered by the statewide manifestation of
racist attitudes. In August 1965 during one of the hottest sum-
mers in Los Angeles, the black community of Watts exploded
into California's most devastating racial incident. It was a six-day
disaster during which nearly ten thousand blacks took to the
streets, stores were looted and burned, cars destroyed, white
passersby beaten, and in the end thirty-four persons were dead.
The businesses that were destroyed were mostly white-owned.
The people who died were mostly black. Ironically, a year
before this event the Urban League had judged Los Angeles the
most desirable city for blacks. The subsequent McCone Commission Report on this riot as well as other analyses made it
clear that housing, unemployment, and police brutality were
major causes. Of equal interest are the claims that this explosion
was a release from boredom and expression of an end, if tempo-
rarily, of powerlessness.[4] The McCone Commission made the
pioneering suggestion that compensatory programs for blacks
be substituted for the slow moving "equality of opportunity"-
type job programs. Beyond that, the McCone Report failed to
be very sensitive and, according to Bayard Rustin, a long-time
national black leader, was very superficial in its analysis of the
roots of the riot. Yet Los Angeles Mayor Samuel Yorty and
Governor Ronald Reagan did practically nothing in response to
the McCone Report. The federal government did initiate a few
programs in Watts that affected a small percentage of the community's population.[5]

Another event that was probably prompted in part by Proposition 14 and which has already been discussed was the organization in 1966 of the Black Panther party. Black people's feelings
toward the police might have alone brought about a Watts riot
and the birth of the Panthers, but the passage of Proposition 14
could hardly have been oil on troubled waters.

There were other developments involving California blacks
(as well as whites) that were associated with the militants and
left-wing groups. Some of these were high drama but difficult to
measure in terms of popular support by all blacks in the state. In
the sixties and seventies concerned blacks and whites joined in a
movement to publicize the lives of blacks in prisons. A few of

these blacks quickly became the center of attention, none more so than George Jackson, whose prison writings found a pub-~~Ph.D.~~ lisher. He received special attention from Angela Davis, a young black woman who was well known by this time as an avowed ~~in philosophy~~ Marxist and whose hiring and firing at UCLA had caused much notoriety.

In 1970 in a courthouse in San Rafael, Marin County, George Jackson's younger brother, Jonathan, and several other blacks attempted to rescue some black prisoners in the courtroom. They took white hostages with them in order to bargain for the freedom of George Jackson. The effort ended in disaster, with several whites and blacks dead, including young Jackson. It was alleged that Angela Davis had supplied Jackson with guns, fully knowing they would be used in the Marin courthouse. She disappeared but was captured in the East months later. There ensued a tremendous campaign in California and throughout the country to free her, in which the small Communist party and the Black Panthers participated. She was a member of both organizations. After a trial in San Jose, she was acquitted. George Jackson, in a cloudy series of events, later was killed in a shoot-out in jail in what some charged was a planned assassination.

While dramatic scenarios of confrontation were being played out with their symbolic significance for white and black Californians, less volatile developments were taking place that would have consequences of more lasting character. Between 1960 and 1970 the state's black population grew from nearly 900,000 to 1,400,000. A charismatic black, the tall and slim Ronald Dellums, who had served on the Berkeley city council, ran for Congress in 1970 as a Democrat and, with the voting power given him by the coalitions of blacks and whites created during the Free Speech Movement in Berkeley, won a seat as the second black in the House of Representatives. Dellums came by his leadership abilities naturally. His father and uncle were active members of the pioneering black union, the Brotherhood of Sleeping Car Porters. Two years later, Yvonne Burke left her seat in the California Assembly to run successfully for a congressional seat in Washington, where she joined the two other members of the black contingent from California in the House of Representatives. That same year, 1972, Julian

Dixon took Burke's place in the Assembly, and still another new black face appeared in the Assembly from the Los Angeles area, Frank Holoman. That same year Dymally left the Assembly to become lieutenant governor under Edmund G. (Jerry) Brown, Jr.

However, it was not Dymally who was the first black to win statewide office in California. In 1970 in an exciting race against a very conservative incumbent, Max Rafferty, Wilson Riles had become the first black state superintendent of public instruction in California. This position he had sought as an educator rather than as a politician.

Such efforts at black power also achieved results in city elections. Cities such as Richmond, San Bernardino, Oakland, Berkeley, Seaside, and Stockton were electing black city councilmen by now, and in Berkeley black Warren Widener was elected mayor in 1971. In Los Angeles, where blacks cast seventeen percent of the votes, former police officer and city councilman Thomas Bradley, a well-known black leader, became the mayor in 1973. Born on a cotton farm in Texas, Bradley and his parents had moved to Los Angeles when he was a small child. Upon graduation from high school he entered UCLA on an athletic scholarship and later, while working in the police department, earned a law degree. His election victory over the incumbent mayor Sam Yorty was marked by the largest white vote for a black candidate in any American city. In that same year, the largely black city of Compton saw Doris A. Davis elected mayor. In the Bay Area a second black mayor was elected in 1977 when Lionel Wilson gained that office in Oakland through a coalition of conservative and radical blacks, most particularly the Panthers. The list of blacks holding elective public office as judges and members of boards of education as well as lawmakers is extensive and can best be appreciated by a glance at the latest edition of the *National Roster of Black Elected Officials.* In spite of the surge of black elected officials in the 1960s and 1970s, it is useful to remember that none of these twentieth-century personalities was the first black elected to office in California. Nearly a hundred years earlier, in 1888, Edward Duplex, a New Haven, Connecticut, gold-rush-era migrant, was elected the mayor of the little town of Wheatland in Yuba County. He was the town barber.[6]

CHAPTER SIX

The Uncertain Seventies

T HE PERIOD BETWEEN the gold rush of 1849 and the 1970s saw great changes take place in the Afro-American communities of California. For decades the number of blacks hovered at about one percent of the state's population. In the twentieth century it rose slowly until today (1979), following accelerated growth, it is close to eight percent. In the nineteenth century black males persistently outnumbered black females, but in the 1970s balance has occurred. What has persisted is the tendency for blacks to avoid agricultural labor. They became a city people even in counties where the cities were small. Although there always were some black farm owners they have remained few; in 1970 they numbered little more than 35,000 out of more than 1,400,000, and it is not certain that all of them were actually farmers.[1]

For decades, even where blacks were relatively numerous, they were the "invisible men," but that too has changed in California as elsewhere. White racism is weakened, but continues to live in subtle and unconscious ways. As a result, many problems persist in California for black people. Solutions are complicated by honest as well as dishonest differences among people of all colors. These differences are highlighted by the problem of de facto segregation of the schools. In other words, does "unintentional" segregation absolve a community from the need to do something about it?

The current efforts at desegregating the Los Angeles schools are a classic case, and the outcome will be watched nationally. These efforts came about because the American Civil Liberties Union (ACLU) entered the desegregation struggle in Los Angeles and filed a suit in the name of a Mary Crawford in 1968. This produced in 1970 the decision of Judge Alfred Gitelson which led to the busing of students. Negative reactions came swiftly from Mayor Samuel Yorty, Governor Ronald Reagan, and even President Richard M. Nixon. Los Angeles school officials claimed that busing 240,000 children would cost forty million dollars. The ACLU disputed this figure. The decision went back to the courts and Judge Gitelson was defeated for re-election in 1970.[2] To second-guess the conclusion of this decades-long struggle is hazardous. However, one can be certain that as long as blacks feel that separateness represents inequality, and the evidence still supports this view, the desegregation struggle will continue. It will end when blacks feel, as white minorities felt in many eastern big cities in the past, that the preponderance of their particular ethnic group in any school is simply a sign of residence and not discrimination.

The tide of rising expectations among blacks in the 1960s swept through all phases of American life, eventually reaching the exclusive world of the medical schools. In 1969 this movement brought about an affirmative action program in student admissions at the medical school on the Davis campus of the University of California. Under this program sixteen admissions were reserved for minority students out of a hundred openings each year. Allan Bakke, a white civil engineer in his thirties, applied for admission to the Davis medical school in 1973 and again in 1974 and was rejected both times. He concluded that he had been discriminated against because he was white and that he would have been admitted to the Davis medical school but for its affirmative action program.

Bakke took his case to the courts, where his position was upheld by the California Supreme Court. At issue was the constitutionality of the Davis affirmative action program. Among blacks there was divided counsel on whether the university should defend its affirmative action program before the Supreme Court of the United States. They rightly feared that a negative decision by the court, which was widely regarded as a conservative court, would have harmful effects on affirmative action programs throughout the nation. In the end the university appealed to the highest court in the land. After a period of intense uneasiness marked by many demonstrations against Bakke in California as well as across the nation, the Supreme Court on June 28, 1978, handed down a five-to-four decision in favor of Allan Bakke. At the same time, however, the court softened its decision with kind words for affirmative action programs. Such programs would remain legal so long as race was not the sole criterion in granting admission. The Bakke decision put Bakke into medical school, but whether it has kept blacks out of medical schools and comparable professional institutions remains to be seen. The admissions policies of the major professional centers of learning will flesh out the true meaning of the Bakke decision.

While the controversies continue, black cultural visibility rises. Afro-American communities in the state support more than two dozen locally published newspapers. Under various names, Afro-American historical societies have been organized, largely with middle-class black support. In Oakland, a well publicized annual event called Black Film Makers Hall of Fame was organized in the 1970s to bring together national black film talent and honor distinguished performers in much the same manner as Hollywood honors its own in the "Oscar" and "Emmy" award ceremonies.

Only slightly less visible than these glamour events was the almost three hundred percent increase in the number of black school teachers, administrators, and other professionals between 1960 and 1970. The black college student population registered a sharp rise in the same decade. Californians were probably most aware of the black presence through blacks' entry into every home by way of television commercials and the performances of many highly visible newscasters.

The glitter of the theatre, sports, and political talent of California blacks gives pride to the Afro-American community and commands respect from the white community, but deep problems remain. There is need for more trained black professionals in medicine and law. The world of engineering and architecture is still too white. But the greatest need is for many more blacks in the most active and stable parts of the American economy. Here, California blacks, with few exceptions, are generally behind, as they are in the rest of the economy. Black businesses have achieved an uncertain foothold in spite of some notable successes in the insurance and undertaking sectors. They are still struggling for survival in the construction industry in spite of some assistance from the federally funded Small Business Administration (SBA). Looming in the background as a pressure on all these problems are the great numbers of teenage and young blacks without skills or attractive employment. The aftermath of the Watts riot produced many programs that did some good, but when viewed in perspective, they did not go deep enough nor did they endure.

The long-range value of the SBA to black business still remains to be assessed. Information is fragmentary and breakdowns of California data elusive. In an April 1, 1978, *New Republic* article on the SBA, the writer thought the benefits to blacks were clouded by reports that some black businesses received loans they did not need while other black businesses needed loans and did not receive them. Furthermore, there is troubling evidence that black firms are often fronts for white businesses which use this device to get federal aid.

To encourage blacks to stand upon their own feet, to avoid the temptation of shortcuts to wealth, and to safeguard their integrity, the Reverend Jesse Jackson, the charismatic black leader of People United to Save Humanity (PUSH), is conducting an inspirational program throughout the nation to persuade young blacks to develop basic skills regardless of real or fancied obstacles. His slogan is "Black Is Dutiful." However, if the controlling forces of white and black society do not provide the material and psychological underpinnings to his efforts, his work will produce meager results. *Newsweek* reported in August 1975 that by conservative estimate, ten years after the Watts riot, forty percent of young blacks in the area were unemployed. They were without work in spite of an expenditure of four hundred million dollars in Watts which produced a long-needed medical center, an industrial park (the largest plant there employs 250 workers), some government buildings, and a few supermarkets.

EPILOGUE

THE VICTORY OF THE property tax initiative, Proposition 13, and the defeat of Lieutenant Governor Mervyn Dymally and Yvonne Brathwaite Burke for attorney general in the state's elections of 1978 have disturbed California blacks. In retrospect, the defeat of these black candidates seems to have been almost inevitable. The climate created by the passage of Proposition 13, which drastically reduced the revenue generated by the property tax, threatened the re-election of Jerry Brown, but his adroit political footwork saved him handsomely. The distance that Brown maintained in his relationship with Dymally, his lieutenant governor, when Dymally had his public relations troubles, stood Brown in good stead but was a mortal blow to Dymally. Furthermore, the lieutenant governor was not able to share in the image of a frugal public official which Brown had created for himself as soon as Proposition 13 had carried.

Congresswoman Burke had an equally difficult problem. Her opponent, state senator George Deukmejian, was the author of a bill favorable to the death penalty which fitted the mood of Californians in that election year. His bill, Proposition 7, won even more handsomely than he did when he defeated the otherwise politically attractive Burke.

These defeats, however, did not seriously impair the visibility of California's black politicians. Californians continued to see the serene visages of Wilson Riles and Thomas Bradley and the intensity of Ronald Dellums, and they continued to hear the sparkling articulations of Willie Brown. The California political climate would have to undergo drastic and disastrous changes before their presences could be submerged. Evidence of their resiliency is the recent appointment of Yvonne Burke to a vacancy on the Los Angeles County Board of Supervisors.

The effect of Proposition 13 is another matter. The surgery that this new law is requiring on the financial resources of local government will have a harmful effect on minorities in education and in locally funded social services. Barring a reversal of mood by the public, which is not at the moment on the horizon, this harmful effect will deepen in the coming years. There may also be some ironical results as Proposition 13 works its way into local government. There is already the beginning of a flight of white local government employees at the upper levels towards private employment. At the moment many positions are remaining unfilled, but black white-collar workers and professionals may find jobs in local government as a consequence of this situation.

Black progress in the last two decades in California has been impressive in developing leaders, professional people, scholars, and skilled artisans. More blacks than ever before have become conscious of their future and their potentiality. What may prove to be the greatest black victory of the last two decades is the acceptance by majority whites of the belief that life in the United States will be richer and more secure with blacks as full participants.

SUGGESTED READINGS

THE RESEARCH AND WRITING of black history in California is still in its early stages of development. The sheer quantity of the materials in the East and the South gives historical writing on the Afro-American experience in these other regions a clear advantage. Western materials are much fewer in number and are more deeply imbedded in the conventional sources. This is especially true for the nineteenth century and the first quarter of the twentieth century. The sources noted in this essay are those which are reasonably accessible.

The first publication of importance that attempts an overview of California black history is the 1919 work of Delilah Beasley, *The Negro Trail Blazers of California* (Los Angeles: n.p., 1919). Not written by a trained historian, poorly edited and with many errors, it still stands as immensely useful because of the leads to further research. Beasley interviewed many nineteenth-century families and recorded important materials, much of her information taken from the occasionally faulty memories of old-timers. A more recent survey is Kenneth Goode's *California's Black Pioneers* (Santa Barbara: McNally and Loftin, 1974). There is useful material in Goode's book, but it also contains too much general California history and adds little to our knowledge about the period between the gold rush and the 1930s. Jack D. Forbes's *Afro-Americans in the Far West: A Handbook for Educators* (Berkeley: Far West Laboratory for Educational Research and Development, 1969) is a very general work with a strong cultural emphasis. Forbes has done research on the pre-gold rush blacks, and his book is strong in that area, but it also reflects the absence of research in the 1870–1930 period.

As for special topics, the situation in black history is better. Two comprehensive works have recently appeared, which detail educational developments: Charles M. Wollenberg, *All Deliberate Speed: Segregation and Exclusion in California Schools, 1855–1975* (Berkeley: University of California Press, 1976), and

Irving G. Hendrick, *The Education of Non-Whites in California, 1849-1970* (San Francisco: R. and E. Research Associates, 1977). Both works include the experiences of other California minorities. The civil rights struggle for a century is discussed in a useful article by James A. Fisher, "The Political Development of the Black Community in California, 1850-1950," *California Historical Quarterly,* I (1971), 256-266.

The only comprehensive study of gold rush blacks is Rudolph M. Lapp's *Blacks in Gold Rush California* (New Haven: Yale University Press, 1977). It describes the full range of the experiences of this first significant migration of blacks to the West from their departures in the East until the period of pre-Civil War community building and civil rights struggles. The book makes abbreviated use of three articles written by the same author: "The Negro in Gold Rush California," *Journal of Negro History,* XLIX (1964), 81-98; "Negro Rights Activities in Gold Rush California," *California Historical Society Quarterly,* XLV (1966), 3-20; "Jeremiah B. Sanderson: Early California Negro Leader," *Journal of Negro History,* LIII (1968), 321-333.

In recent years some research has been done on nineteenth-century San Francisco and the Bay Area. These works include Francis N. Lortie, *San Francisco's Black Community, 1870-1890* (San Francisco: R. and E. Research Associates, 1973), and James A. Fisher, "The Struggle for Negro Testimony in California, 1851-1863," *Southern California Quarterly,* LI (1969), 313-324. There are also a few unpublished theses for the same period and they are noted in the above article by Fisher.

Twentieth-century materials are more abundant, especially for the period from 1930 to the 1970s, and for southern as well as northern California. Two excellent pieces by Lawrence B. de de Graaf bring Los Angeles black history into sharp focus: *Negro Migration to Los Angeles, 1930-1950* (San Francisco: R. and E. Research Associates, 1974), and "The City of Black Angels: Emergence of the Los Angeles Ghetto, 1890-1930," *Pacific Historical Review,* XXXIX (1970), 323-352. Black migration to the Bay Area during World War II is treated in Charles S. Johnson's *The Negro War Worker in San Francisco* (San Francisco: n.p., 1944). A useful article on the same topic is Cy W. Record, "Willie Stokes at the Golden Gate," *The Crisis,* LVI (1949),

175-179, 187. Information on discrimination in industry in the West for the same period can be found in Herbert R. Northrup's *Organized Labor and the Negro* (New York: Harper and Brothers, 1944). Also useful is Edward E. France's *Some Aspects of the Migration of the Negro to the San Francisco Bay Area since 1940* (Palo Alto: R. and E. Research Associates, 1974).

For students and general readers who wish to pursue more detailed reading on blacks in films and in the film industry, the British cinema historian Peter Noble's *The Negro in Films* (London: Skelton Robinson, 1948) is a fine work. It has a chapter on blacks in British and European films which includes a great deal about Paul Robeson. However, the most recent and probably most comprehensive study of the American Negro in films and film-making is Thomas Cripp's *Slow Fade to Black* (New York: Oxford University Press, 1977).

With help from the *Reader's Guide to Periodical Literature*, *Ebony* magazine can be a fruitful source of profiles on many California blacks in public life after 1945. Material on the small town and rural California blacks may exist but it thus far lies buried in hitherto unexamined sources. However, Walter Goldschmidt's *As You Sow* (New York: Harcourt, Brace and Co., 1947), an agricultural study, provides some useful data.

Published material on the post–World War II civil rights revolution and the black nationalist period that followed it is of uneven quality, although in great abundance, but little of it is exclusively devoted to California. The history of the NAACP in the West can also be found in the definitive work on CORE by August Meier and Elliott Rudwick, *CORE: A Study in the Civil Rights Movement, 1942-1968* (Urbana: University of Illinois Press, 1973). The book also contains considerable information on CORE activities in the West. A useful article on Garveyism in the West is Emory Tolbert's "Outpost Garveyism and the UNIA Rank and File," *Journal of Black Studies*, V (1975), 233-253.

Recent manifestations of black nationalism, such as the Black Panthers, are reported in works like Reginald Major's *A Panther Is a Black Cat* (New York: W. Morrow, 1971), a sympathetic account which is Bay Area–oriented and by a black author. Don A. Schancke's *The Panther Paradox* (New York: D. McKay Co., 1970) is more detached but concentrates on Eldridge Cleaver for whom the white author developed an admiration. The push by blacks in California for black studies still needs its historian, but some details can be found in Nick Aaron Ford, *Black Studies* (Port Washington, N.Y.: National Universities Publication, Kennikat Press, 1973); August Meier, Elliott Rudwick, and Francis L. Broderick, *Black Protest Thought in the Twentieth Century* (2nd ed., Indianapolis: Bobbs-Merrill, 1971); and Harry Edwards, *Black Students* (New York: Free Press, 1970).

NOTES

CHAPTER ONE

1. Jack D. Forbes, "Black Pioneers: The Spanish-Speaking Afro-Americans of the Southwest, *Phylon*, XXVII (1966), 241-244.

2. Juan Bautista Alvarado to Allen B. Light, Jan. 22, 1839, Hayes Documents, Part 2, San Diego Archives, transcript, Bancroft Library.

3. Zoeth Skinner Eldredge, *The Beginnings of San Francisco* (2 vols., San Francisco: Eldredge, 1912), II, 526-529.

4. *California Star*, Aug. 25, 1847.

5. Rudolph M. Lapp, *Blacks in Gold Rush California* (New Haven: Yale University Press, 1977), 12-48.

6. Ibid., 166-185.

7. Ibid., 192.

8. Ibid., 210-219.

9. Richard H. Orton, *Records of California Men in the War of the Rebellion* (Sacramento: State Printing Office, 1890), passim.

10. Charles M. Wollenberg, *All Deliberate Speed* (Berkeley: University of California Press, 1976), 24-25.

11. Forbes, "Black Pioneers," 245.

12. Lapp, *Blacks in Gold Rush California*, 118-125.

CHAPTER TWO

1. *Sacramento Daily Union*, Oct. 25, 1865; *Stockton Weekly Independent*, Jan. 30, 1869; *Elevator*, Jan. 8, 1869.

2. Rudolph M. Lapp, *Blacks in Gold Rush California* (New Haven: Yale University Press, 1977), 92-93.

3. Roy W. Cloud, *Education in California* (Stanford: Stanford University Press, 1952), 45.

4. Charles M. Wollenberg, *All Deliberate Speed* (Berkeley: University of California Press, 1976), 21-24.

5. *Appeal*, Nov. 24, 1977; March 30, 1878; April, 1879.

6. *Elevator,* Oct. 15, 1869.

7. Oscar Lewis and Carroll D. Hall, *Bonanza Inn* (New York: Knopf, 1939), 31, 32, 58.

8. J. Alexander Somerville, *Man of Color* (Los Angeles: Lorrin L. Morrison, 1949), 71.

CHAPTER THREE

1. *Crisis,* Aug. 1913.

2. Kenneth Goode, *California's Black Pioneers* (Santa Barbara: McNally and Loftin, 1974), 111.

3. Charles S. Johnon, *The Negro in American Civilization* (New York: Henry Holt & Co., 1930), 78-79.

4. Goode, *California's Black Pioneers,* 89.

5. James A. Fisher, "The Political Development of the Black Community in California, 1850-1950," *California Historical Quarterly* L (1971), 261.

6. Thomas Cripps, *Slow Fade to Black* (New York: Oxford University Press, 1977), 74-89.

7. Quoted in Peter Noble, *The Negro in Films* (London: Skelton Robinson, 1948), 104.

CHAPTER FOUR

1. Lawrence B. de Graaf, *Negro Migration to Los Angeles, 1930-1950* (San Francisco: R. and E. Research Associates, 1974), 86.

2. Lawrence B. de Graaf, "The City of Black Angels: Emergence of the Los Angeles Ghetto, 1890-1930," *Pacific Historical Review,* XXXIX (1970), 327.

3. Wilson Record, *Race and Radicalism* (Ithaca: Cornell University Press, 1964), 95-97, 161-165.

4. De Graaf, *Negro Migration,* 114-121.

5. Roi Ottley, *New World A-Coming* (Cleveland: World Publishing Co., 1945), 320-331.

6. Roger Daniels and Spencer C. Olin, Jr., eds., *Racism in California* (New York: Macmillan, 1972), 266-280.

7. *Shelley* v. *Kramer,* 334 U.S. 1 (1948).

8. W. W. Robinson, *Lawyers of Los Angeles* (Los Angeles: Los Angeles Bar Association, 1959), 168-169).

CHAPTER FIVE

1. August Meier and Elliott Rudwick, *CORE* (Urbana: University of Illinois Press, 1975), 251-252.

2. Robert Brustein, *Revolution As Theatre* (New York: Liveright, 1971), 13-28.

3. *New York Times,* Jan. 5, 1976.

4. Frederick J. Hacker, M.D., "What the McCone Commission Didn't See," *Frontier,* XVII (March 1966), 10-15.

5. Roger Daniels and Spencer C. Olin, Jr., eds., *Racism in California* (New York: Macmillan, 1972), 29-39.

6. Rudolph M. Lapp, *Blacks in Gold Rush California* (New Haven: Yale University Press, 1977), 259.

CHAPTER SIX

1. U.S. Department of Commerce, Bureau of the Census, *California, 1970,* Vol. I, p. 93.

2. Charles M. Wollenberg, *All Deliberate Speed* (Berkeley: University of California Press, 1976), 158-160.